GOD
AND THE CELEBRATION OF LIFE

GOD and the Celebration of LIFE

Harvey H. Potthoff

RAND McNALLY & COMPANY
CHICAGO • NEW YORK • SAN FRANCISCO

All Bible quotations are from the Revised Standard Version, unless otherwise noted.

Library of Congress Catalog Card Number: 69-16637
First printing: February, 1969

To

DR. *and* MRS. CARL J. POTTHOFF

Is man alone in the universe or not? — MIGUEL UNAMUNO

For God alone my soul waits in silence, for my hope is from him. — PSALMS 62:5

The modern world has lost God and is seeking him[1] . . . I hazard the prophecy that that religion will conquer which can render clear to popular understanding some eternal greatness incarnate in the passage of temporal fact.[2] . . . Religion will not regain its old power until it can face change in the same spirit as does science. Its principles may be eternal, but the expression of those principles requires continual development.[3]

---

[1] A. N. Whitehead, *Religion in the Making* (New York, The Macmillan Company, 1926), p. 74.

[2] A. N. Whitehead, *Adventure of Ideas* (New York, The Macmillan Company, 1933), p. 41. Used by permission of the publisher.

[3] A. N. Whitehead, *Science and the Modern World* (New York, The Macmillan Company, 1929), p. 270. Used by permission of the publisher.

Preface

IF YOU ARE seriously interested in the question of how God is meaningful in contemporary life, this book has been written with you in mind. It is for students, pastors, and laymen who are seeking to understand some of the main currents of contemporary theological discussion.

Theologians have a way of writing books for other theologians. It has long seemed to me that more books should be written for the thoughtful person who has honest questions about religion and the meaning of God in his own life and the lives of others, but who is not familiar with technical theological language. This book is an attempt to write for this audience.

It is obvious that there is much ferment these days in religious thought. The scientific age has brought a revolution in our understanding of man and the universe. Technology and sociological movements are bringing profound changes to the conditions under which we do our living. It is inevitable that traditional expressions of religion should be called into question. The result involves widespread confusion. While some would call us back to "the old-time religion," others affirm that

"God is dead" or that modern man has outgrown the need for the supports and sanctions of religion. Still others affirm that we have indeed outgrown various religious beliefs and practices, but that our present need is for a more mature form of religion, tenable within contemporary experience and knowledge.

This book is one person's attempt to see what lies beneath the seemingly confused theological situation of our time. It focuses on two central theological issues—the reality of God and the meaning of God for our lives. Many persons are rethinking ideas of God previously held. There are honest doubts. Sometimes the church speaks meaningfully on these matters. However, many persons both inside and outside the church do not find the church speaking in depth to the doubts and questions they are experiencing. This book is for persons, both inside and outside the church, who are searching for what they believe a living religion might bring to them, but who are dissatisfied with much traditional religion. This book, then, is not for those who are convinced they have found the answers. It is for those who are honestly seeking. It is for those persons who experience the haunting sense that life can and should mean more than it does mean to the masses of men.

There is a practical dimension to this book. Its purpose is not to prove or disprove the existence of God in an abstract sort of way. Rather, it deals with the question of how we may speak meaningfully of God and live in the awareness of God's reality as we go about our daily activities, doing our work, relating to other persons, facing moral dilemmas, making decisions, functioning as citizens, wrestling with the perennial problems of life and death, seeking meaning in our existence. It is the privilege of every person to affirm or deny the reality of God or to take the agnostic position. But it is humanly impossible to avoid the experiences or issues which for many persons raise the question of God. The question of what we are finally up against in life and death is ever with us in one form or other, and we make some kind of response.

Thus, the purpose of this book is not to convince or to convert. Its basic purpose is to share one man's view of the tremendous importance of mature religion in our time, and to indicate terms on which such religion is possible.

There are many resources available to us as we seek to move toward a new day in theological thought. This book is an invitation to look beneath and beyond the traditional religious structures and languages in quest of a living faith which calls men to be truly whole and to accept and celebrate life in its fullness. It is intended to communicate a vision of hope.

HARVEY H. POTTHOFF
Denver, Colorado

Table of Contents

ASKING THE GOD-QUESTION

Part One

1.
The Whole Person Asks the God-Question

MANY BOOKS on God begin with the question: "Does God exist?" Then follow various arguments for the existence or nonexistence of God, together with claims as to the nature of God.

In this book we shall follow a different procedure. We shall begin by looking at man's life and asking, "What is it to be alive as a human being?" "What are the thoughts, feelings, problems, and aspirations which attend being alive as a person?" We shall try to lay bare those dimensions of life which raise the God-question. By following this procedure, we shall perhaps come to a more relevant way of asking about God. We shall try to show how the question of God is a meaningful question in relation to our day-by-day experience.

The Basic Awareness of Being

There are some aspects of our existence that are so fundamental we scarcely ever speak of them at all. We take them for granted. Such is the basic awareness of *actually being* and *participating in being.* The infant experiencing discomfort and satisfaction, the adolescent struggling with problems of identity, the middle-aged person seeking a mature view of life and the universe even as he carries on his day-by-day responsibilities, the older person of declining health and vitality yearning for a sense of dignity and worth in his existence, all manifest in varied ways the elemental and the fundamental awareness of *being.*

The awareness of being is a two-sided matter. As it develops it involves a sense of one's own unique being. I am I. *I* breathe, *I* experience various bodily functions, *I* suffer, enjoy, and in varied ways announce to the world that *I* am here. *I am.* But along with the sense of I-ness is *the sense of being related.* On its most elemental level this is the sense of participating in being. Around me are various persons and objects. I am related to them. But together, we all participate in being. To be something or someone is to be related and to participate in being.

The awareness of being comes to involve the sense of being derived from a past and moving toward a future even as one experiences the immediacy of a present in which past and future come to focus. To be a self is to be a center of thought, feeling, action, aspiration—in relationship. We live and move and have our being in a space-time matrix in which we are both unique and related.

Thus, beneath the surface of our lives is the awareness of being. This awareness is so basic to our existence as persons that we seldom reflect upon it. It is there, woven into the very texture of our existence. It is a dimension of our living which must be taken into account as we seek an understanding and a style of life which celebrates life in its wholeness. Somewhere along the way the question rises, "Can we speak meaningfully of the being in which we participate?" It may be that the most fruitful place at which to begin inquiry about God is with our own existence—in its uniqueness and relatedness.

The Pain of Being Human

To be alive as a human being is to experience varied kinds of pain. Life is inherently demanding. In every age there have been those who have pointed to the pain of human life. Thus, in the Devas' song in Buddhist literature we read:

> *We are the voices of the wandering wind,*
> *Which moan for rest, and rest can never find,*
> *Lo, as the wind is, so is mortal life—*
> *A moan, a sigh, a sob, a strife.*

The author of the Book of Job affirmed that "man is born to trouble as the sparks fly upward" (Job 5:7). Henry Thoreau wrote, "The mass of men lead lives of quiet desperation." Ian MacLaren said, "Be kind to every person you meet. He is having a hard time." Writing from his existentialist perspective, Jean-Paul Sarte has referred to man as "a useless passion." That life is inescapably painful is the testimony of men in all ages and of varied philosophies.

Fortunately, man has the capacity to reflect upon his own experience. In that reflection he may come to some insight into the how and why of his hurting. In this discovery he stands on the threshold of deliverance from slavery to pain. He continues to suffer, but in a different way. Even in the midst of his hurting he is able to ask, "What sort of meaning will this aspect of my experience have for my total experience as a person?" Thus, it is important that we look more carefully into the hurting we experience as human beings.

There is the *pain of frustration.*

To be human is to experience needs, wishes, aspirations. But these are met and fulfilled only in part. To be alive as a person is to be thwarted in many matters about which we are deeply concerned. Someone has written, "You gave me wings to fly, then took away my sky." Life often seems to mock us in creating desires which are destined to be satisfied only in part. The hunger for love and beauty and knowledge and success and fulfillment often is unmet, or satisfied in only limited measure. To be human is to know the pain of frustration.

There is the *pain of conflict*.

We experience the ambivalent character of our inner lives and the conflict of values. The person of yesterday quarrels with the person of today. We experience the struggle of good and evil within ourselves, the pain of conscience, the agony of guilt, the struggle between the actual and ideal. We experience the conflict of deep-rooted impulses with each other and with socially approved mores and with authoritarian figures. We experience the tensions and conflicts inherent in human relationships—sometimes loving and hating at the same time. Conflict is written into the life process.

To be human is to experience the *pain of loneliness*.

There is the loneliness of being uniquely oneself—which means being different from others. Some of life's profoundest experiences are essentially solitary, lonely experiences. There is a loneliness in the competitive aspect of life. But most painful of all is the feeling of not being meaningfully related. The feelings of not being understood or cared about, of not being able to communicate with persons around us, of having no cause or purpose to give life depth or direction, add up to the devastating loneliness of not being meaningfully related. It appears that our own natures are such, and the nature of the universe in which we live is such, that some measure of frustration, conflict, and loneliness is inescapable.

To be human is to experience the *pain of growth*.

To be human is to participate in an operation of cosmic dimensions—growth. At the points where we have ceased to grow, we have begun to die. But to grow is to outgrow, and that is painful. To grow is to move beyond infantile self-centeredness and preoccupation with self; it is to move into a larger world of meaning and commitment—but this is painful. It is to leave behind some ideas and concepts and customs and loyalties in which we have found security and satisfaction, as we move into larger understandings and more inclusive worlds of experience.

In our time, the demand for human growth is taking on new and awesome dimensions. Through developments in various sciences, including genetics, man is now called upon to make decisions which were once assumed to be God's alone. As never before, man has it in his power to have a voice in determining what sort of creature man shall become. Obviously, this kind of decision-making calls for a new kind of man—one who is forever outgrowing his past as he moves into new worlds of understanding and sensitivity and concern. There is excitement and joy in the growth which is called for, but there is also profound pain. It is a part of the price of being truly human in this kind of world in this time.

To be human is to experience the *pain of facing deterioration and death.*

The Psalmist said, "The years of our life are threescore and ten, or even by reason of strength fourscore; yet their span is but toil and trouble; they are soon gone, and we fly away" (PSALMS 90:10). We have learned to prolong life, but there appears to be no final escape from physical suffering, deterioration, and death as part of the human story. We live within limitations of time and strength. Many relationships must be broken, work left unfinished, dreams unrealized. Linked with all this is the pain of knowing that the world will get along without us. Most painful of all is the knowledge that those nearest and dearest to us are subject to suffering, deterioration, and death. If being human involves the awareness of our participation in being, it also involves living with "the threat of nonbeing."

To be a human creature of intelligence and sensitivity in a world which is dynamic, interrelated, and ever in process of becoming something new is to experience profound pain. This is a part of the dignity and agony of man.

Out of the heart of life's pain come questions of deepest human significance. Whence comes *courage* to carry on and move ahead? For what kind of *meaning* may man appropriately hope? In the midst of life's fragmentation and tearing-apart processes, how can we move toward *wholeness* and *fulfillment?* We are so constituted that we seek courage, meaning, wholeness, and fulfillment. Without them we do not truly live. But in the midst of life we are forever coming up against limitations which seem to deny us what we most deeply desire and need. *Is there meaning and hope at the limiting points of human experience?* In one way or other we all wrestle with this crucial question.

The Wonder of Being Human

Even as man experiences pain, he also experiences the wonder-ful.

The processes of being born as a human creature are awesome. The universe into which we are born is full of wonders. As G. K. Chesterton put it, the world will never starve for want of wonders but only for want of wonder. The human creature and the experience of being alive as a human being have wondrous dimensions.

While man experiences the pain of frustration, he also knows the joy that comes in *satisfaction of some needs and the achievement of some goals*. A measure of frustration seems to be required for full appreciation of life's most rewarding values. Some goodness, beauty, understanding come into most lives; these are intrinsic values that justify the human venture. There is a measure of fulfillment in feeling that through one's work he participates in the unending work of creation.

Out of the experience of conflict there sometimes comes *the wonder of emerging identity and wholeness.*

Though life involves struggle, it also affords the conditions for achieving selfhood, coming to a sense of dignity and worth as a person. To have survived some of the deeper struggles of the soul, to go beyond conflicts which seemed devastating, winning some victory of the spirit, is a wondrous experience.

The pain of loneliness can be unspeakably difficult, but life also affords *the wonder of meaningful relationships.*

Some loneliness seems to be the price of being meaningfully related—with persons of sensitive spirit, with the good earth and growing things, with positive interests, with communities and causes of significance. To feel that one is a part of all that he meets, so that he keeps going beyond himself in his relationships, is one of the wonders of being alive as a person. Friendship and loyalty and love are positive facts of human experience.

Though *there is pain in much of human growth, there is even more of wonder in it.*

To be born and to grow through various stages of life into a human being capable of mature love is to participate in the most wonderful of all realities. To grow in response to a great idea or ideal which has grasped us; to grow beyond infantile self-centeredness into a caring, creating person; to go beyond loss and failure and broken dreams in openness to life's healing resources—and come at last to feel that life is indeed potential for meaning and hope—is to know the full wonder of human life.

It is in *the capacity for self-transcendence and situation-transcendence* that the wonder of man's existence comes to highest expression.

It is in the capacity of going beyond himself and beyond the situation at hand that man's spiritual dimension is revealed. The will to create even in suffering, to seek excellence, to see the present in terms of what might be or ought to be, to laugh at oneself with a wholesome perspective, to endure disappointment with equanimity because one sees life whole, to worship in gladness of heart recognizing a greatness that transcends man's finiteness, is to express a wonder which is distinctively man's.

Though there is the pain of physical suffering, deterioration, and death, *it is also given man to exemplify a unique dignity and hope in the presence of "the last enemies."*

There are bonds of sympathy and understanding and caring which can be experienced only in the presence of suffering and death. Only man knows that he will die. But with that knowledge there is also the capacity for a vision of one's relation to the whole of being. Death is not an isolated event. In the mystery of things, life and death, destruction and creation, transiency and rebirth are wondrously interrelated. It is given to man to know these truths.

Because of the capacities of mind and spirit with which he has been endowed, man is able to experience *the depth of meaning in this moment* which comes through memory, anticipation, and loyalty to self-transcending values.

This moment is truly now, but its bare is-ness is redeemed for meaning as man brings his memories, hopes, and self-transcending loyalties to bear upon it. Man, by nature, is a hoping, vision-seeing, goal-seeking creature. He is not only pushed by forces behind and around him; he is lured by ideas, ideals, possibilities, challenges. Man is born for *becoming* in relation to *the whole of being*—and therein lies not only the pain, but the wonder of his existence. The celebration of life is the celebration of life in its wholeness—including the pain and the wonder of being human. It is the celebration of being alive as a human being *now*—in relation to all that participates in being. Man, indeed, is born for a unique status in the order of creation. A child of nature, he brings a new dimension to nature.

The Decision to Be Human

The purpose of life is to live. The purpose of being a human being is to be truly human and to grow in the human qualities. This seems obvious. Yet, we often miss the point that this is what life is really all about.

Nicolas Berdyaev asked, ". . . is that being to whom the future belongs to be called man?" Perhaps this is the most crucial question of our time, when the future of the human race is at stake. Man is significantly involved in determining his own destiny. This is a part of the pain and wonder of being human. Yet, man does not always make the courageous or creative decision. He sometimes chooses a style of life which avoids or rejects the pain of sensitive caring and creative living.

Albert Camus wrote, "There is only one really serious philosophical problem: that is suicide." While relatively few perssons commit suicide in a physical sense, multitudes of persons choose to cut off or destroy certain aspects of experience which involve the profounder thoughts, feelings, and relationships. We can commit emotional suicide in varied ways, by seeking to avoid the pain and responsibilities of being sensitively, lovingly human. The will to affirm and celebrate life in the fullness of its pain and wonder is not easily come by.

In the presence of life's demands it is possible to follow the paths of flight, fight, or fulfillment.

In the quest for escape, one may turn to such obvious devices as drugs, excessive activity, immersion in the sensual, or life-denying religion. It is possible to play a role other than that involving responsible maturity: a subhuman animal, a dependent child, a sick adult, an efficient but unquestioning cog in a machine. Sometimes individuals seek escape from the demands of a fully human existence by endeavoring to play God, rejecting or denying the limitations of finitude.

Frustrated by the demands of life, some persons lash out or

fight back in anger. Dr. Karl Menninger, among others, has suggested that there is no more urgent question than this: How can we encourage love and diminish hate? Margaret Mead has pointed out that persons can be reared to "trust and love and experiment and create, or to fear and hate and conform. . . ."[1] Destructiveness, complaining, exploitiveness can become ways of life. A great deal of the anger and destructiveness in the world can be traced back to the feeling that one is not adequate for meeting the demands of life. Frustration may lead to flight or fight.

Fortunately, there is still another possibility for man as he confronts the pain and wonder of being human. He can face life honestly. He can recognize that his life must be lived within limitations. No person lives under ideal circumstances. Life is offered to each individual on different terms. Life comes to mean somewhat different things to different persons. Yet, each human being can seek such fulfillment as is possible and appropriate to his situation. It is not a matter of having everything or nothing. Life is the art of the possible. To seek the possibilities in each situation for sensitive, appreciative, creative living is to seek the way of life fulfillment and celebration.

Man is indeed a wondrous creature in his potentialities. But he also has the capability of rejecting the venture of life in its mature wholeness. Seeking a style of life in terms of which he can function reasonably well, man sometimes settles for a partial existence. He carries on day after day, but the note of depth is missing. He dies as a complete human being. Thus, he misses the mark of what he was born to be—and "sin" in its root sense means "to miss the mark."

In this context of thought, Berdyaev's question comes with force: ". . . is that being to whom the future belongs to be called man?" Perhaps a part of the answer lies within ourselves in our decision to be or not to be truly human. Man has a measure of personal choice in how he responds to the human situation.

Man's Hoping and the Question of God

In the presence of our deepest problems (including those of internal frustration and conflict, tangled human relationships, the pain of feeling that one is not meaningfully related), we inevitably experience ambivalent feelings about being alive as a person. We experience the inner propulsion *to move ahead into life* and *to grow;* at the same time we experience the desire to *shrink back* from the painful demands of maturing life. Thus, a continuing struggle goes on in the depths of our being. What sorts of persons we become and what life comes to mean to us depends in large measure on the resolution of this struggle.

To be able to participate in life most fully, to celebrate life in its wholeness, requires that we move through a series of crises in infancy, childhood, and adulthood. These crises have been variously analyzed. One such analysis is that of Dr. Erik Erikson who speaks of the healthy personality in relation to crises through which come basic trust (versus basic mistrust), the autonomous will (versus shame and doubt), initiative (versus diffusion), intimacy (versus self-absorption), generativity (ver-guilt), industry (versus inferiority), identity (versus identity sus stagnation), integrity (versus despair and disgust).[2] To understand ourselves and the mystery of human life, we must understand the forward-thrust of life and also our own mixed feelings as we experience the motive of growth and the motive of shrinking back. The pain of life's crises sometimes seems more than we can bear.

Thus, it appears to be the destiny of man to leave the paradise of innocence and security and enter a world of toil and struggle, conflict and frustration, knowledge of good and evil, the joy and pain of responsible decision and action. Yet we simultaneously affirm and reject this destiny. We are problems to ourselves. We wish to grow up and we do not wish to grow up. We desire freedom and we seek escape from its demands.

We yearn for authentic selfhood and fear it. We are drawn toward relationships which are essential to wholeness, yet we pull away from the self-giving they entail. To grow toward wholeness or to settle for a more secure but partial existence—this is the question.

It is out of this profound struggle of our inner lives that the questions of courage and meaning reappear. It is in the inner arena where the conflicting motives of growth and shrinking back are being experienced that we wrestle with our fears and anxieties, our sense of futility and meaninglessness, our feelings of fragmentation, alienation, and uncertainty as to who we are. Is there a courage adequate for dealing with our fears, a significance which overcomes the sense of emptiness, a wholeness which gathers up the fragmentation and brokenness of our lives? To reply in the negative is to say that the final story of life is one of meaninglessness and possibly despair. To reply with at least a qualified "yes" is to acknowledge a measure of hope. Of such crucial importance is this matter of hope and hoping that we must look at it more carefully.

In his book *Das Prinzip der Hoffnung* (The Principle of Hope), Ernst Bloch develops an analysis of man as "the creature who hopes." Along with a growing number of contemporary thinkers, Bloch believes that we do not see man in his wholeness unless we see him as one who is future-oriented. Human existence involves an "infatuation with the possible."[3] In a similar vein, Gordon Allport insists that an adequate interpretation of human personality reckons with the "becoming" dimension of the human creature. We grow as persons and become more authentically human, not simply through opportunistic adjustments and tribal molding, but through our hoping and our response to the unattained goal. Man's hoping reveals him as a creature whose "passion for integrity and a meaningful relation to the whole of Being" may be his most distinctive capacity.[4] Any adequate philosophy of life must reckon with man's capacity for living in expectation of the not-yet.

Sometimes we hope for specific things. Sometimes our hoping is more of an openness to life's undefined possibilities. In either case, the person of hope is one who lives in a world of open doors and anticipations. Life, for the person of hope, has not stopped nor is it a prison of monotony. It is experienced as involving frontiers, the future, the new. Hope is an orientation to life in its dynamic wholeness.

We have said that out of the experience of life's deepest pains and in the midst of the struggle between the growth and shrinking back motives, man asks the questions of courage and meaning and wholeness. These are the questions which express our hoping. Hope is the outreach of our inner lives for courage, meaning, and wholeness. Hope brings the spirit of man to life. It is the reality which transforms resigned existence to positive life affirmation.

Hope is not something we bring into being by an act of will. A man cannot simply say, "I shall be hopeful today" and be assured that hope will appear. Its roots go deeper. Hope is grounded in trust, in a basic confidence. Only he who lives with and in a basic trust is free to hope. Lacking this trust, he builds defenses, wears masks, and shuts himself off from life-giving resources. Trust is the precondition of hope.

We come, then, to the conclusion that a basic trusting and hoping are essential for being alive as a person. In the midst of frustration and conflict, there is the hope for inner unity and harmony. In the midst of destructive and tangled human relationships, there is the hope for mutually enhancing and fulfilling relationships. In the midst of feelings of alienation and emptiness, there is the hope for a meaningful relationship to the whole of being. In the midst of ignorance, greed, war, prejudice, and poverty there is the hope for an order of life in which increasing numbers of persons may experience a more satisfying and creative life. The spirit of man is nurtured in hope. Hope is living in expectation of the not-yet. In the midst of the pain and wonder of human existence, we live by hope grounded in trust.

Since hoping is essential to being meaningfully alive, the question of *what we trust in and hope for* becomes the central issue of our lives. A person's character reflects his trusting and his hoping. What, then, do we take into account in our trusting and hoping? When human resources appear to be exhausted and we confront mystery, is there a basis for hope? When we come to what seem to be the limits of human life, in what do we trust and for what do we hope? These are questions which rise out of life itself.

Questions of this sort are ultimately religious in character. We trust and hope in many things. We find courage and meaning through devotion to many things. But in the midst of life we keep coming to the question, "Is there that in which we may trust and hope *at the limits of life?*" When human knowledge and power have taken us as far as they can in given situations, is there something more to be taken into account? Is there *a more* which inspires and justifies hope throughout our experience of the pain and wonder of being alive—and when we come to the end of that experience? Rudolph Bultmann has defined faith as freedom from the past and openness to the future. Is there a ground of faith, so defined, at the limiting points of life?

To ask that question is to ask the God-question. Historically the word "God" has referred to the ultimate ground of hope. The whole person asks this question. It is partly an intellectual question, but it is more. It is partly a question relating to our feelings about life, but it is more. It is partly a question relating to our attitudes and actions in specific situations, but it is more. It is a question involving our whole selves in relation to the whole of being. It is a question which gathers up our orientation to life in its wholeness. We conclude, then, that the God-question is not simply the philosophical question, "Does God exist?" It is a question having to do with the meaningfulness of life itself and the ultimate ground of hope. To speak of God is to speak of hope grounded in faith. To believe in God is to accept, affirm, and celebrate life in its wholeness—even when we confront the limitations of human finitude.

Because the God-question rises out of life itself as we experience the pain and wonder of being human, and because it has to do with the question of the ground of man's most enduring hope, it is a *profoundly meaningful question*. In the long run it may be the *most* meaningful and urgent question in man's experience.

2.
The Experiment of Getting Along Without God

THERE ARE those who are convinced that man's most enduring hope lies within himself. According to this view, scientific man no longer needs the supports and sanctions once found in the transcendent or the supernatural. Indeed, it is only as man recognizes that his salvation lies in his own hands that he is free to live most creatively. Whereas life may raise the question of God, life also gives the answer that man no longer needs the crutch of traditional religion. In man himself are the needed resources for a meaningful life as he works for the achievement of ideals and a more humane society.

In his book *The Philosophy of Humanism*, Corliss Lamont gives a clear statement of this point of view:

> Humanism is the viewpoint that men have but one life to lead and should make the most of it in terms of creative work and happiness; that human happiness is its own justification and requires no sanction or support from supernatural sources; that in any case the supernatural, usually conceived of in the form of heavenly gods or immortal heavens, does not exist; and that human beings,

> using their own intelligence and cooperating liberally with one another, can build an enduring citadel of peace and beauty upon this earth. . . . Humanism asserts that man's own reason and efforts are man's best and, indeed, only hope; and that man's refusal to recognize this point is one of the chief causes of his failures throughout history.[1]

For the most part, humanists believe that the word "God" is so inextricably interwoven with the idea of other-worldly supernaturalism that it is best to cease using the word God at all. The presupposition seems to be that modern man must choose between an outmoded supernaturalism, on the one hand, or a philosophy of humanism, on the other. Technically, agnosticism means the denial of the possibility of knowledge. Atheism refers to the denial of the existence of deity. While some humanists are atheistic, others would simply hold that knowledge of the existence of deity is not possible. The humanist insists that he can find nothing in his experience which refers to, points to, or establishes the reality of God.

Life Affirmation Without God

Humanism is a philosophy of life affirmation and life celebration without God. It recognizes both the pain and wonder of human existence and says "yes" to the human venture. It seeks the fullest life possible for all men. It seeks to recognize the dignity of the individual and his responsibility for helping create a better society. The humanist is open to the new understandings of man and the universe which come through the sciences. He believes that in the application of human intelligence, goodwill, and hard work directed toward ideal ends, man may indeed move toward a more satisfying and fruitful life. The basis of humanistic hope is thus in man himself.

There have been many variations on the theme of humanism. We shall look at several well-known expressions of this philosophy. They vary in detail, but they share a common confidence in man. They agree that much traditional religion has hampered rather than helped man in his quest for the fullest possible life. The time has come for man to bring his own powers to bear upon the problems of being human without recourse to extrahuman agencies associated with the religions. In so doing, emancipation will come and a new day for mankind.

One of the classic expositions of humanist philosophy is Bertrand Russell's essay, *A Free Man's Worship*. Russell develops the thesis that man must choose between the worship of amoral and destructive power, on the one hand, or devotion to his own ideals of human good and human welfare, on the other. The first is the worship of the slave; the second is the free man's worship.

Russell holds that "the nonhuman world is unworthy of our worship." Man is subject to vast powers of nature which will in the end destroy him. He writes:

> Brief and powerless is Man's life; on him and all his race the slow, sure doom falls pitiless and dark. Blind to good and evil, reckless of destruction, omnipotent matter rolls on its relentless way; for Man, condemned today to lose his dearest, tomorrow himself to pass through the gate of darkness, it remains only to cherish, ere yet the blow falls, the lofty thoughts that ennoble his little day; disdaining the coward terrors of the slave of Fate, to worship at the shrine his own hands have built . . . to preserve a mind free from the wanton tyranny that rules his outward life. . . ."[2]

In this philosophy we are called to a realistic facing of our situation. We are called to exercise our capacity to live nobly in service to our fellowmen and in quest of a more humane world. It is a philosophy stressing the potential dignity of man in a universe of destructive power. Russell's essay seeks to link intellectual honesty with deep concern for human values. However, it finds little in the universe which is enduringly supportive of the values man cherishes most.

In 1933 a group of distinguished Americans signed a document called *The Humanist Manifesto*. It was a relatively brief statement setting forth the conviction that the time has come for revision in religious thinking. Unlike Russell's essay, the manifesto did not dwell on the destructive character of the natural powers to which man is subject. It expressed the conviction that the universe is self-existing and not created; that man is a part of nature, having emerged "as the result of a continuous process." However, like Russell's essay, the manifesto held that "the nature of the universe depicted by modern science makes unacceptable any supernatural or cosmic guarantees of human values." Thus, man is called to turn from the old attitudes involved in prayer and worship to cooperative efforts in the promotion of social well-being. The manifesto insisted that the distinction between the sacred and the secular no longer can be maintained; that religion (without God) "consists of those actions, purposes, and experiences which are humanly significant." The manifesto was clearly life-affirming in its emphasis, insisting that "religion must work increasingly for joy in living."

Some persons may be surprised that humanists would use the word "religion" to apply to their philosophy of life. As a matter of fact, humanists are not of one mind on this point. Some would hold that modern man no longer needs religion. Others would say that man does indeed need a religion of the human spirit—but without recourse to any God save that which man himself creates in his ideal-projecting.

In the 1920's and 1930's a number of books appeared setting forth the humanist philosophy.[3] It is interesting to recall that these were the years when the so-called modernist-fundamentalist controversy within the churches was at its height. One wonders whether some of the views being expressed in that controversy might have influenced certain writers to set forth the humanistic alternative to both fundamentalism and modernism.

The humanist writers of this period differed somewhat in the measure of support they believed man may find in his non-human environment, but all agreed that human hope lies in man himself. Max Carl Otto put it this way:

> What noble things might be accomplished if we recognized in our insistence upon cosmic companionship a deflection of the desire for fellowship with our kind, and in the craving for transcendental support of our ideals a distortion of our deep interest in human well-being and progress! . . . It is thus a constructive social suggestion that we endeavor to give up, as the basis of our desire to win a satisfactory life, the quest for the companionship with a being behind or within the fleeting aspect of nature; that we assume the universe to be indifferent towards the human venture that means everything to us; that we acknowledge ourselves to be adrift in infinite space on our little earth, the sole custodians of our ideals.[4]

Speaking directly to the question of God, R. W. Sellars wrote:

> Either a reality corresponding to the God-idea is at the center of reality in a directing, planning way or there is no such reality. In the latter case man is left to work out his own salvation as best he can with a fairly stable planet underneath his feet. His is the adventure and the goal. . . . It is not my intention to brush aside all the arguments used by Christians and other theists to show that

> the God-idea does have application. I must content myself with saying that none of these arguments have seemed to philosophers very convincing.[5]

For Sellars, the dismissal of God from serious consideration led not to discouragement but to a religion which "says yea to life here and now . . . the religion of courage and purpose and transforming energy."[6]

In 1934 John Dewey published his widely-read book, *A Common Faith.* In this work Dewey emphasized the importance of ideals in human experience. Ideals exercise a creative influence on man, profoundly affecting his conduct. He said that "any activity pursued in behalf of an ideal end against obstacles and in spite of threats of personal loss because of conviction of its general and enduring value is religious in quality."[7] Dewey suggested that while he would not insist on the use of the word "God," it would be appropriate to use that term in reference to "a unification of ideal values that is essentially imaginative in origin when the imagination supervenes in conduct. . . ."[8] Again he wrote, "It is this *active* relation between ideal and actual to which I would give the name 'God.' "[9] Dewey held that ideals are generated and supported by "forces in nature and society." In that statement he moved toward a form of religious naturalism. Yet, his emphasis is upon man's capacity to project ideals and to work toward their realization. The God of whom Dewey writes presumably would not exist apart from man in his ideal-projecting function. Thus, Dewey's position is strongly humanistic in its orientation.

In recent years we have heard relatively little of those persons whose works have just been cited, with the possible exceptions of Bertrand Russell and John Dewey. However, we have been hearing a great deal about what Hazel Barnes calls "humanistic existentialism." To a consideration of that form of humanism we now turn.

Humanistic Existentialism

The forms of humanism which we have considered thus far represent, for the most part, reactions against supernaturalistic theology, theologies based on speculation about the nature of the universe, and theologies of resignation. By way of contrast to such theologies, the humanism we have been considering has stressed a "this worldly" philosophy, appealing to the authority of contemporary experience and scientific method. It teaches that man can create a better life and a better world. In man's rational and moral powers lies his greatest hope.

Humanistic existentialism has much in common with the earlier humanisms. However, while they were primarily occupied with attacking supernaturalistic and metaphysical interpretations of religion, humanistic existentialism focuses its attacks on deterministic and fatalistic theories of man. At the heart of humanistic existentialism is the doctrine that "every man is free, but most men, fearing the consequences and the responsibilities of freedom, refuse to acknowledge its presence in themselves and would deny it to others."[10]

The most significant possibilities for man are related to his *freedom to decide*. As Nicola Abbagnano put it, "Freedom is possibility."

Albert Camus, Jean-Paul Sartre, and Simone de Beauvoir are representative humanistic existentialists. For our present purposes we may consider the humanistic perspective of Camus. He was convinced of the absurdity of the human situation. Subject to suffering and death, man is alone in a universe with which he does not have communication. The absurdity of the human situation is manifest as man brings his longing for happiness and rational unity to a world of "unreasonable silence." If the world has a meaning which transcends it, man cannot know this. There are no compelling arguments for the existence of God. Hence, the person of good faith must face the question as to whether he can live with what he knows and with that alone. Philosophy's fundamental question is whether life is worth the trouble of being lived.

Under these circumstances, according to Camus, one can give way to despair or recognize that life can be worthwhile even in a meaningless world. One can stand up to the absurd, exercise one's freedom in dignity, and give himself in sensitivity and passion to life, with life understood as a succession of presents, without reference to the future.

Thus, Camus calls us to life affirmation without God. He appeals to man's freedom and capacity for decision. He calls for an existence of intensity in the present, marked by good faith, sensitivity to the needs of others, limited and realistic expectations of life. Camus tells us that we can win our way to authentic selfhood and inner freedom as we make our own decision to affirm life in a meaningless world.

If the earlier humanisms of which we spoke found hope in man's rational, moral, and ideal-projecting powers, humanistic existentialism finds man's hope in his own freedom to make decisions.

Humanism and the "Death of God" Movement

Three names are most frequently associated with the "death of God" movement: Thomas J. J. Altizer, Gabriel Vahanian, and William Hamilton. All three think of themselves as being in the Christian tradition, all three speak of the "death of God," and all three insist that the Christian church must reckon with the death of God; contemporary theology needs to accept the truth of the death of God if it is to fulfill its purpose in this time.

However, it is important to recognize that these three persons speak of the death of God with different meanings.

Altizer holds that the transcendent God, once known as Creator and Lord, became immanent in Jesus and died in his crucifixion. Thus God ". . . has emptied himself of his original sovereignty and transcendence."[11] ". . . Jesus Christ is the name of the God who has become fully and totally incarnate. . . ."[12] It is Altizer's contention that the contemporary Christian can have nothing to do with a static, transcendent God, but must give his commitment to the Christ who is ". . . the full embodiment of love, . . . the pure actuality of the total moment . . . the totality of the moment before us . . . who draws us into the fullness of life and the world."[13] We are called, then, to "give ourselves totally to the world, to affirm the fullness and the immediacy of the present moment as the life and the energy of Christ."[14] Although Altizer uses theological language and reveals an interest in mysticism in his writings, his final appeal appears to be for a commitment not too different from that of the socially concerned humanist.

Vahanian speaks of the "death of God" in quite another sense, as "a cultural phenomenon." Modern man, who thinks rather exclusively in "this worldly" terms and in terms of immanence, has lost his sense of the true, transcendent God. The cultural changes we have been experiencing have been attended by the loss of the experience of the holy. For Vahanian the death of God as a cultural phenomenon is not something to be celebrated; it is a fact to be recognized. We have fallen into a religiosity which is neither pagan nor Christian. In our emphasis on the immanence of God, we have lost the vision of the "Wholly Other" who judges us and in relationship to whom we understand who we are. Thus, although Vahanian speaks of the death of God, he represents a position very different from that of Altizer and cannot be regarded as an exponent of the humanistic philosophy we have been considering in this chapter. He writes, " 'To kill God is to become god oneself': this is the meaning of the transition from radical monotheism to radical immanentism which has taken place in western culture."[15] It is Vahanian's conviction that the God of biblical faith has profound significance for modern man, but in the midst of modern cultural changes, man has lost his vision of that God.

William Hamilton is convinced that traditional ideas of God have lost their meaning for multitudes of contemporary persons. Furthermore, he doubts that the transcendent creator God of traditional faith exists or ever did exist. In the past men have practiced a religion in which they turned to this God as "fulfiller of needs or solver of problems."

The time has come, Hamilton believes, when men should realistically face the fact that "there is no God-shaped blank within man," that God is not necessary to avoid despair or self-righteousness. The time has come for a new optimism concerning man and his possibilities, for turning from "the cloister to the world" in creative work and service. In so doing man will trust the world, not God, as need-fulfiller and problem-solver. Hamilton writes, "This combination of a certain kind of God-rejection with a certain kind of world affirmation is the point where I join the death of God movement."[16]

Hamilton does not hold that the idea of God can never have significance for modern man. He simply says that the time has passed for thinking of God in the role of fulfiller of needs and solver of problems. It is possible that God may appear some time in another role wherein we will enjoy him and "delight in his presence." Thus, we live in a time of "waiting for God," searching for an appropriate language and style. In the meantime "we have a place to be . . . in the world, in the city, with both the needy neighbor and the enemy" in obedience to Jesus Christ.

This brief summary of some of the leading ideas of Altizer, Vahanian, and Hamilton indicates that there are important differences among them. All are aware of secularizing processes in the modern world and that these processes are deeply influencing the religious perspectives of thoughtful men. Altizer and Hamilton are particularly outspoken in insisting that the otherworldly God has no place of relevance in the modern world. Man must live out his commitment in a life of service *in* the world in obedience to Jesus Christ. In view of man's difficulty in speaking meaningfully of God in our time, it behooves man to get on with the business of being responsibly present in the world, drawing on his own intelligence and strengths in the light of his obedience to Christ. It is evident that there are strongly humanistic dimensions to the thought of both Altizer and Hamilton.

An Evaluation of the Humanistic Position

The humanist wishes to be intellectually honest even if that means surrendering long-cherished beliefs. He wishes to function as a mature, responsible person in the world of today. He wishes to have a part in creating a society in which more persons will have the opportunity for a meaningful life. He is a person of hope, and he believes that man's greatest hope lies in himself.

Because of the integrity and idealism which characterize humanism as described, many intelligent and sensitive persons are attracted to this philosophy. Perhaps an increasing number of persons are adopting it as their own philosophy. It deals with the here and now. It seems to make unnecessary the giving of attention to theological ideas of dubious validity. It encourages men to get on with the business of living in a creative and useful way. One wishes that more persons committed to the organized religions shared in the social vision and concern of many humanists!

But we do well to examine some of the presuppositions of humanism and to see at what price its seeming advantages are gained. Humanism takes an extremely optimistic view of man. The presupposition seems to be that by virtue of his rational and moral powers, man is equipped to bring in the better world which is desired. Man is capable of creating a better man and a better society. We do, indeed, have growing evidence that man has potentialities which have gone unrecognized. Man is indeed a wondrous creature in the order of nature. But we also have mounting evidence that greed and destructiveness are a part of the human picture. Man is his own biggest problem. As a creature born to a measure of frustration and conflict, man does not always respond in creative and fulfilling ways. Facing this fact, the major religions of the world have insisted that man's salvation does not lie wholly in himself. Man's hope for becoming more of a whole person lies in a transformation issuing in greater inner harmony. This transformation involves a discipline and a way oriented toward a more-than-human reality. Herein is one of the major issues to be reckoned with in evaluating the humanist position as an adequate philosophy for our time. What sort of creature is man? Does the creative life to which humanism summons man require a transformation which man alone cannot bring about?

A second issue on which an evaluation of humanism must turn has to do with the limited world in which humanism chooses to live. Society becomes the "frame of orientation and devotion." Yet, society itself is set within a larger matrix of events. Nature includes but transcends society. Man in his varied human relationships and institutions derives his life from a deeper source than society alone. It would appear that an adequate philosophy for our time would aim at an understanding of man's relationship to reality in its *wholeness*. The perspective of humanism is commendable and inadequate all at the same time.

We have noted that some humanists speak of "religious humanism." The question of the appropriateness of that designation may now be raised. Does humanism, in fact, fulfill the basic functions of religion? We shall have occasion to speak of the religious response in greater detail in the next chapter. At this point it is well to note that there does, indeed, seem to be much of a religious quality in the humanist way of life. There is a dedication to self-transcending values. There is reverence for life and respect for the dignity of the individual. There is a recognition that man's life is not his own to do with as he will; even as he derives much from society, so he is called to give himself to social goals and purposes. Humanism is a form of life affirmation and celebration.

It is evident that some of the functions of religion are fulfilled in the humanistic way of life. In his human relationships and in his devotion to self-transcending values man may find acceptance, a measure of forgiveness, the warmth and support of sustaining fellowship, the challenge of goals. There is the inspiration which comes from knowing that the meaning of life is not measured in terms of one's life span; one's influence goes on through the causes to which he has dedicated himself. One may celebrate major events of life in the fellowship of those with whom one is united in bonds of memory, hope, and caring. An enriching sense of history and tradition is possible within the framework of humanistic thinking. Let no one, then, depreciate the humanistic way of life as being superficial or devoid of reverence for life. There are many persons dedicated to humanism who exemplify depth and reverence in their lives.

Yet, historically, religion has meant something more than this. It has meant the experience of a power, presence, and purpose from beyond man. It has had to do with the coming of a courage and meaning and wholeness through divine working. The person of religion has usually believed that in the midst of life he was finally accountable to a divine source of life. His hope has been derived not only from man, but supremely through the divine.

Thus, the question persists as to whether something important is not left out in humanism. The word "God" has represented the "something more" of which humanism is reluctant to speak. It is God who provides the ultimate "frame of orientation and devotion" within which the person of religion lives and aspires. The person of religion testifies that in his relationship to God there comes a courage, meaning, and wholeness which man and society alone cannot provide. John Herman Randall, Jr. has put it this way:

> The great religions have offered men a transcendent or 'spiritual' ideal that goes beyond their finite ends, and raises them above the mere search for material goods, for social goods, even for others. They have given him an aim for living that can stand in the face of outward failure, and an incentive for striving on to victory against insuperable odds. . . . They have counseled feeding the hungry and healing the sick; but they have had a vision beyond such easy winning. Men need for their fullest satisfaction such a transcendent ideal—more than abolishing poverty, more than establishing a just social order, more than bringing peace upon earth. If they have it, they can wrest victory out of the very jaws of defeat. For in disaster finite ends are revealed as finite, and man sees himself in his true stature as a 'spiritual' being, with a vision that can transcend the limits of time and space and the petty conditions of existence. Man can behold what he finds most real in the universe and commit himself to its demands. For religious men, this ultimate which eludes definition and yet is shadowed forth even now in existence, is conceived as Divine. This object of faith and vision they call God.[17]

To assert that through their faith in God some men have found resources of strength and meaning does not prove that God, as they conceive him, actually exists. It may well be that some persons would like to affirm the reality of God but cannot do so in honesty. Thus, they turn to the humanistic philosophy. At this point we would simply say that before dismissing tálk of God as being meaningless, or referring to something which in the nature of the case cannot be verified, we need to look further into the life of religion.

The humanistic positions we have been looking at all represent reactions against supernaturalistic-dualistic world views, gods who function in miraculous ways, truth-claims based on presumably infallible authority, religions which promise absolute truth or absolute assurance, religions which relieve man of his actual responsibilities in the world. The humanistic philosophy is set forth as the logical alternative to such views and religions. That there may be still other alternatives is not seriously considered by most of the humanistic writers. But if there are other alternatives they need to be given serious consideration. The intellectual respectability of the humanist comes at a very high price. The price is that of leaving vast areas of man's larger environment out of consideration and of forgoing some of the deeper meanings of religion as men have experienced them.

The question then comes: Is there a serious alternative to humanism for modern man? Can the words "religion" and "God" suggest significant meanings or realities for the person who lives in a secular world, who assumes the validity of scientific methodologies, and who perceives his life to be set in a universe which is dynamic, interrelated, ever becoming, and possibly self-sufficient?

It is evident that we must probe more deeply into the meaning of religion and the meaning of God in human experience. Once we relinquish the idea of religion as something basically magical or metatechnological, what meaning does religion have, if any? And if we relinquish the idea of God as miracle-worker, the filler of gaps in our knowledge, the guarantor that our wishes will be fulfilled here or hereafter, what sorts of meaning, if any, can the God-idea have? We shall give attention to these fundamental matters in succeeding chapters. The fact that modern man has outgrown certain ideas of religion and certain concepts of God does not necessarily mean that he has outgrown the need for religion in all forms. To grow is to outgrow. This principle applies in religion as well as in other dimensions of life.

3.

Beyond Humanism: Human Hope and the Vision of God

THUS FAR we have said that to be alive as a human being is to experience pain and potentiality, frustration and fulfillment. In the presence of life's difficulties we experience the motives of shrinking back and growing. On the one hand, we may engage in mechanisms of escape, denial, evasion, regression. On the other hand, we may affirm existence, seeking to move further and deeper into life, discovering and expressing its possibilities ever more fully. It is not simply a case of either-or. Our feelings about life are ambivalent, and our responses are likely to involve both shrinking back and growth dimensions.

Our need is for a style of life in which we may grow toward wholeness in relation to all reality. The nature of our hope and hoping becomes a crucial matter in relation to what life means to us and the kinds of persons we become. As we hope, so we respond to life.

We have noted that there are those who seek to follow the way of life affirmation without God. We have called this the way of humanism. From this perspective man finds his ultimate hope in himself and in society. His guiding vision is that of a new man in a new social order. The humanistic way of life seeks intellectual integrity even if it must come at the price of giving up consolations and promises often associated with religion. It is a way of human concern for justice in the relationships of men and for a society in which through human effort all persons will have greater opportunity for a fruitful and satisfying existence.

In this chapter we go on to consider the meaning of religion in the life of man, thinking of religion as *that way of life in which man finds his ultimate hope in God.* Religion, so understood, may gather up the hope that springs from humanistic understanding, but goes beyond this to affirm that life itself springs from a divine source, and in that divine source is man's *ultimate* hope.

Regardless of what one may think of religion, he cannot escape the fact that there are religious persons. There are persons who profess to have come to a vision of God and in the light of that vision to have found all things have changed meanings. They see themselves, other people, daily experiences, the crises of life, the pain and wonder of being human in a new perspective of hope. In this chapter we shall make inquiry into religious attitudes and responses. First, we shall consider the approach of those who observe and study religion, endeavoring to discover its role or function in the lives of individuals and groups. Then we shall consider the meaning of religion for the person who professes it. In the process we shall raise the question of the meaning of the God-idea within the framework of religious life and thought. We shall raise the question of the meaning of God within the framework of the religious perspective and life.

Where we find religious persons we normally find: (a) human beings involved in the problems and possibilities of human existence; (b) persons experiencing and/or aspiring after what they believe to be the divine; (c) persons giving some expression to their vision and experiences of the divine in myth or sacred story or other theological symbol; (d) persons acting out their experience of the divine in what is regarded as sacred rite; (e) persons adopting or confessing a way of life deemed to be in harmony with the divine.

Religion, of course, takes many forms. There is great variation in belief and practice. Persons vary in the degree to which they express the religious responses. Religion functions in various ways in different times and settings. But the deeper meanings of religion are always to be understood in relationship to what persons are experiencing, what they are fearing, loving, trusting, valuing, hoping. Religious belief and ritual are oriented toward what men believe to be their ultimate hope. Religion is man's response to the vision of God expressed in belief, rite, and life-style. John Hutchison writes:

> Closely related to rite is myth, or sacred story. The life values that are acted out in rite are sung out in myth. Whether myth or ritual is first is indeed a chicken-and-egg question. They must be regarded as two expressions of the same concern, namely of the values by which a man or community lives and declares life meaningful.[1]

Before probing more deeply into the religious response to life it should be acknowledged that the worst and the best in man has been expressed in the name of religion. At times religion nurtures ignorance, prejudice, rigid conformity to the status quo, hostility, and destruction. There is such a thing as "sick religion," wherein religion is used to escape, distort, or deny reality factors in one's situation. It is a tragic fact that on many occasions progress and new knowledge have been resisted in the name of some religious orthodoxy. At other times religion nurtures the most creative dimensions of man, inspiring the search for truth, nobility of action, and dedication to the highest values.

In this book we are seeking an honest appraisal of how religion functions in the lives of men. We shall then be in a better position to consider its potential role in the contemporary world. If religion is outmoded, we ought to face that fact and turn to more legitimate and fruitful human concerns. If, on the other hand, there is sound reason to believe that religion does have important, abiding functions in human life, we ought to try to define those functions and seek ways of achieving maturity in religious thought and practice. Perhaps in the process we will be driven to ask the God-question in new ways.

The Observer's View of Religion

A growing understanding of religion involves a study from two perspectives: that of the external observer and that of the religious person himself. Religious phenomena are studied by anthropologists, psychologists, sociologists, philosophers, and many others. These persons have much to say about the role or function of religion in human experience in various cultures. It is important that we listen to what they have to say. But it is equally important that we listen to the individual who has something to say about what his religion *means to him*. There are dimensions of the inner life of meaning not easily probed by the external observer. We need to seek an understanding of religion from both perspectives. We need to understand languages *about* religion and languages *of* religion.

Among the major theories which have been advanced by observers as to the function of religion are these: (1) Religion has an integrating function in the life of the individual. It affords assurance and support, enabling persons to meet the demoralizing experiences of life in hope, transforming and/or sublimating fear, grief, guilt, hunger, sexual crisis, and so on. (2) Religion functions in nurturing and expressing what are regarded as useful and intrinsically satisfying experiences of the divine, such as the mystical experience, the sense of the presence of God, the awareness of the "holy." (3) Religion functions as agent of social control, providing sanction for mores and traditions of societies. (4) Religion functions in the integration of social groups, providing, through beliefs and practices, means for celebrating the shared values of the group. (5) Religion functions in relationship to other institutions of society, serving a uniting, supportive, and critical function in relation to the family, government, culture.

There is evidence to indicate that religion functions in all these ways at various times and in various settings. In some primitive situations religion is believed to function in providing explanations (often in mythical form) of why things are as they are; in providing escape from difficult or threatening situations; in inducing the controlling power or powers to give man what he wants.

Sometimes the attempt is made to distinguish between lower and higher religions, primitive and civilized religions, immature and more mature forms of religion. E. A. Burtt distinguishes between the religions of simpler societies (simpler in social organization, language, tools, economic functioning) and the religions of more complex societies.[2] He holds that in the more primitive religions found in simpler societies, the stress is upon the meeting of insistent needs through winning the favor of divine powers. In the presence of threatening and mysterious powers man seeks divine help for survival. In the more civilized religions, the concern is more for a blessedness which transcends the immediate satisfaction of desire—a relationship to the divine which confers dignity on the individual, sometimes effects inner transformations, and directs man's aspirations to ideal ends.

In his widely read book *The Individual and His Religion,* Gordon Allport distinguishes immature and mature forms of religion. Immature religion, he suggests, is largely concerned with magical thinking, self-justification, and creature comfort. By way of contrast, "mature religion is less of a servant, and more of a master, in the economy of the life. No longer goaded and steered exclusively by impulse, fear, wish, it tends rather to control and to direct these motives toward a goal that is no longer determined by mere self-interest."[3] It is extremely important to recognize that religion takes many forms; all religion cannot be fairly judged on the basis of one particular expression of it.

That religion in some form is well-nigh universal seems to be the case. That it has been an unqualified good in the history of mankind clearly is not the case. That men continue to ask questions pertaining to courage and meaning and wholeness seems to be true—and these are the questions to which religion addresses itself. An external observer of the phenomenon of religion cannot help but wonder what directions the religions of man will take in a world of increasing technology and increasing communication among the peoples of the earth. Will they restrict man's perspective and growth, or will they release him for a new and creative chapter in human history?

The Insider's View of Religion

The person of religious faith may or may not be interested in an anthropological, psychological, sociological, or philosophical analysis of religion. But he is profoundly interested in the meaning his faith has *for him*. He speaks out of his inner life and out of his experiences shared with others in a community of faith. If we are to understand the meaning of God in human experience, we must learn to formulate the God-question from the perspective both of the outside observer and of the person of faith.

Just as the whole person asks the question of God, so the

whole person of faith affirms the reality of God in his experience. He does not simply say, "I have an intellectual conviction that God exists." He affirms, "God is present in my life in a saving way." To be sure, he may not use just those words, but he is very likely to affirm in one way or other his personal experience of a more-than-human power and presence in his life.

To understand the meaning of religion it is essential that we try to hear persons who witness to their faith—as they speak of a grace they have experienced, an enduring integrity they have come to trust, a sustaining presence they have come to know, a healing-forgiving-redeeming reality to which they have responded, a call and claim they have come to acknowledge. The person of religious faith is convinced that in the midst of life he is dealing with a more-than-human Sacred Reality, that his ultimate relationship is with a Real-Other who (or which) illuminates and judges all other relationships. The person of religious faith may be deeply interested in the here and now, but he lives with a sense of *what is ultimate, what he keeps coming to* in the midst of life, *what he is finally up against.* Even in the midst of the deepest pain of life he lives in hope, and that hope is grounded in God. Somehow, somewhere the vision of God has come to him. For the person of faith, life in its fullest and most authentic sense is life lived in hopeful response to the vision of God. Writing of the essentially hopeful character of the religious response, William James said, "If any one phrase could gather its [religion's] universal message, that phrase would be 'All is *not* vanity in this Universe, whatever the appearances may suggest.' "[4] The Psalmist affirmed, "For God alone my soul waits in silence, for my hope is from him" (Psalms 62:5). The person of mature religion affirms human life in its wholeness in response to the vision of God. It is God, he is convinced, who ultimately calls man to affirmation and celebration of life. Furthermore, in God are resources in terms of which man is strengthened and undergirded and motivated in that affirmation.

The outsider observing the person of religion may appropriately say, "That person's faith appears to bring morale, meaning, and motivation into his life." The religious person himself may or may not engage in that sort of analysis of his own religious life. But in his worship, trust, and devotion he does, indeed, reveal heightened morale in the face of discouragement, loss, and tragedy; deeper meaning in living; and a motivation to grow toward wholeness in relation to the whole of being. Indeed, his world is changed in the light of the vision by which he lives. The philosopher, George Santayana, wrote, "The vistas it [religion] opens and the mysteries it propounds are another world to live in; and another world to live in—whether we expect ever to pass wholly into it or no—is what we mean by having a religion."[5]

As we read great devotional literature and listen to persons of religious depth speak out of their experience, we discern three recurrent themes which gather around the vision of God: *consolation*, *celebration*, and *challenge*.

The *consolations* of religion include the experience by the man of faith of undergirding strength in times of tribulation, the assurance of God's caring presence and companionship, the promise of forgiveness, the hope that tragedy and evil may be transformed into good, the experience of a peace that passes all understanding. In all known cultures men have found hope through their religions—hope in the presence of demoralizing events, conditions, and experiences which they have believed to be beyond their control. This hope has been grounded in the reality of God, variously conceived.

Out of extensive investigations of religion in various cultures, William H. Bernhardt formulated his conclusion pertaining to this abiding function of religion among those who take it seriously:

> Religious behavior is a complex form of individual and group behavior whereby persons are prepared intellectually and emotionally to meet the non-manipulable aspects of life positively by means of a reinterpretation of the total situation and with the use of various techniques.[6]

Bernhardt insists that the need for religion, so defined, is present in all cultures, including those of highly developed technologies. To function with a maximum of satisfaction and creativity man must come to some working relationship with those aspects of his experience which are demoralizing and also presumably beyond his external control. Although modern man is now able to control many aspects of his experience once regarded as mysterious and uncontrollable, he continues to experience the pain of frustration, conflict, growth, death. New discoveries bring new problems. It is Bernhardt's view that as long as man is finite man in a universe that is both sustaining and threatening, he will need the resources of religion *or their functional equivalent.* In every culture there are those who are able to meet life more positively because of the consolations and inspirations of religion. Many persons who normally reveal little interest in religion seek out the resources of religious faith in times of stress, danger, and tragedy. Historically, religious faith has been one of man's major sources of strength and hope in the presence of life's inevitable, demoralizing experiences.

In the dimension of *celebration,* religion is an expression on the part of the man of faith of values which have been found. Through deliverances which have been experienced, new insights achieved, new meanings appropriated, new hopes fulfilled, men have been enabled to leave some imprisoning past and move into a new present and future. There is good news to be celebrated. Thus, in the languages of religion we find not only the theme of consolation, but the themes of praise, thanksgiving, joy.

In the higher religions the vision of God issues not only in consolation and celebration but also *in challenge*. God summons man to grow, to aspire, to serve, to reach for the unattained ideal or goal, to overcome difficulties, to explore the unknown, to become a new person, to share in the creation of a new world. The individual is not permitted to rest content where he is; he is called to be on his way. His life is not his own to be used as he will. He lives under a call and claim. The vision of God brings a sense of destiny, of a future.

In the sixth chapter of the Book of Isaiah we find a classic expression of one man's religious experience, set forth in dramatic language. There is the vision of God: "Holy, holy, holy is the Lord of hosts; the whole earth is full of his glory." Then comes the shaking awareness of man's own finitude and separation from the holy God: "Woe is me! For I am lost; for I am a man of unclean lips, and I dwell in the midst of a people of unclean lips; for my eyes have seen the King, the Lord of hosts!" Then comes the consoling assurance of cleansing and forgiveness: ". . . your guilt is taken away, and your sin forgiven." And, then, as a climax to this encounter with the living God the words are heard, "Whom shall I send, and who will go for us?" To this call and challenge the prophet replies, "Here I am! Send me."[7]

Not all persons of religious faith profess to come to their awareness and vision of God in the same manner as did Isaiah. Sometimes the vision is said to come much less dramatically in the midst of the commonplace experiences of life. But attendant upon the vision is a similarity of testimony: the sense of finitude, sin, separation from the Sacred Reality; the experience of healing, forgiving, life-giving grace; the summons into the service of God. The person of religious faith lives in the same world as do others. Yet, he sees and experiences that world in a different way. He lives through the pain and wonder of existence with an abiding sense of the worth of life.

Whence Comes the Vision?

Alfred North Whitehead wrote, "I hazard the prophecy that that religion will conquer which can render clear to popular understanding some eternal greatness incarnate in the passage of temporal fact."[8] It is when the vision of an eternal greatness breaks in upon man, putting all things in a new light, opening the possibility for a new existence in hope, calling men into a new life with the force of a cosmic claim, that the word "God" is appropriately spoken.

But whence comes the vision? To this crucial question there is no simple answer. Each person makes his own spiritual pilgrimage. Each has his own story to tell. There is much of mystery in the coming (and the not coming) of the vision of God and the life of faith.

Yet, there are some things we can say. Experiences of dependability, appreciation, and love in one's human relationships often have something to do with the emerging awareness of life's divine dimension. Experiences of some success in dealing with problems have something to do with it. Experiences of incoming strength, healing, and deliverance often bring the conviction of a grace operating in one's life. The movement toward a comprehensive belief system in which the fragments of existence are seen in a pattern of unity and coherence may bring intimations of the eternal and pervasive greatness some men call God. Having significant identification figures (persons of courage, mature love, and religious sensitivity) oftentimes has something to do with the coming of the religious vision. Participation in a community of faith, in which life is celebrated as a gift of God, tends to nurture the life of faith. The dawning of the possibility of deliverance at some point of crisis or of overwhelming sorrow may be attended by the conviction that man is not alone in the universe.

When the external observer of the phenomenon of religion speaks of these matters, he is likely to point to settings, processes, experiences, and relationships which are implicated in the coming of the life of faith and the vision of God. He gives a sensible, naturalistic accounting of it all. But when the religious person himself speaks of these matters he is likely to go further. He may acknowledge the importance of religious training and so on, but he is also likely to speak of *revelation* in some form. The light of God's reality and presence has broken in upon him. He feels that the initiative has been God's and not man's. God has given, not simply some information *about* himself; he has given *himself*. He has come to man in self-disclosure, calling forth a response of trust and devotion. To the person who experiences the vision of an eternal greatness through revealing events, persons, and experiences, arguments for the existence of God may seem superfluous. His knowledge of God appears as a gift. There is a "spiritual perception." Paul wrote, ". . . we look not to the things that are seen but to the things that are unseen; for the things that are seen are transient, but the things that are unseen are eternal" (II CORINTHIANS 4:18).

Some people think of revelation as the divine disclosure of *information* about God: his nature, his will and purpose, his disposition toward man. Others think of revelation not so much as the giving of propositional truths, as *the giving of God himself*: his presence, his power, his grace. In either interpretation, revelation is understood to be God's gift to man.

While the person of religion often appeals to revelation as the primary source of religious truth and insight, the outside observer is likely to be confused by such talk or suspicious of it. At best, the appeal to revelation seems to put religion on a highly subjective basis. At its worst, appeal to revelation opens the door to all sorts of vagaries and preposterous claims. It is one of the tragic facts of religious history that fantastic claims have been made, hard-won knowledge has been denied, inhuman deeds have been committed in the name of "divine revelation."

The person of mature religion is aware of the pitfalls involved in the appeal to revelation. He seeks, therefore, to show how revelation is related to reason and the totality of man's experience. He may insist that the vision of God comes in a variety of ways and that no one way stands alone.

Life Affirmation—With and Without God

In the last two chapters we have considered two ways of life affirmation and celebration—the humanistic and the religious. In the first, man's ultimate hope is found in man and society. In the second, man's ultimate hope is in God. The person of religious faith believes that it is God who calls him to life affirmation and celebration, that life at its best is life celebrated in praise of God.

These two ways of responding to life are not entirely opposed. The sensitive humanist joins hands at many points with the person of mature religious faith. But there is a crucial difference in their respective "frames of orientation and devotion." The person of religious faith endeavors to see life and death in relation to the ultimate mystery which surrounds man. Religion involves the attempt to find identity and meaning in relation to the whole of being. Religious faith appeals to a dimension of ultimacy about which humanism is silent.

4.
The Future of Religion

WHAT IS the future of religion in the modern world? In striking language Dietrich Bonhoeffer insisted that one kind of religion has no future at all with thinking people. That is the immature religion which fills in the gaps in man's knowledge with pious phrases, nurtures dependence, and diverts man's attention from his responsibilities in the world. It is the religion which sharply distinguishes the sacred and the secular, regarding the holy as just a province or segment of real life. It is a religion interested in "cheap grace" rather than obedience in the world. The widespread attention which Bonhoeffer's writings are receiving indicates that he speaks to many persons in our time.[1]

The modern world is committed to science. Religion which is little more than a mythological substitute for science probably has little future with informed persons. Religion which does not presuppose the validity and importance of the scientific enterprise cannot be expected to interest the contemporary mind. Religions which are oriented to the past or to another world have less and less appeal. Religious movements which concern themselves primarily with service-functions already being performed better by secular agencies tend to lose their following. Bonhoeffer was correct. Much of what has gone on in the name of religion has little or no place in a "world come of age."

What, then, can be said about the future of religion? Immature religion probably will continue to have an appeal for many persons. But what about persons who have, in Bonhoeffer's words, "come of age"?

The answer turns on two crucial questions: (1) Does modern man have needs and questions to which religion has a distinctive contemporary relevance? (2) Is there a dimension of reality with which science does not deal directly but which needs to be taken into account if man is to achieve wholeness and hope in his total experience? If these questions are answered in the negative, religion will tend to fade away. If the answer is affirmative, we may reasonably assume that modern man will continue his age-long search for more adequate vehicles through which to express his spiritual aspirations.

At the heart of life is a persistent urge for expression and freedom and fulfillment. Even against great obstacles this urge keeps reasserting itself. Insofar as religion provides interpretations, visions, symbols, fellowships, and other resources for expressing, directing, and acting out the thrust of life toward fulfillment (even in the face of demoralizing experiences), it will play an important role in human experience. Failing to address itself to distinctively religious needs and questions, or failing to provide contemporary modes of thought and worship, it will probably tend to become more and more peripheral in man's concerns.

Modern man seeks an orientation to reality in its wholeness. His need is for new forms of religious expression which enable him to unite intellectual honesty with the profounder feelings and aspirations of the spirit.

Religion and the Pain of Being Human

Historically, religion has enabled man to find hope in the presence of the most devastating human experiences. Frustration, conflict, loneliness, suffering, tragedy, and death have led men to seek religious resources. Religion has provided theological interpretations of these painful realities and offered a hope born of the vision of God. It has provided sustaining communities of faith in which the pivotal experiences of life could be related to the Ultimate Mystery of being. Religion has not always provided answers, but it has provided a "frame of orientation and devotion" in which human events were seen as being significant.

How we answer the question of religion's future depends in considerable measure on how we believe the man of tomorrow will cope with the most demoralizing aspects of his experience. Can the various sciences, arts, and related disciplines take over the significant functions once performed by religion? Do these disciplines say all that can or should be said about man and the whole of which he is a part?

While learning much about many things, man continues to be his own biggest problem. To be human is to experience inner frustrations, conflicts, disharmonies. Man continues to experience the world as both sustaining and threatening. His life span moves toward deterioration and death. Destructive suffering is a fact. The causes are many and complex. But it would be presumptuous to affirm that increase of knowledge and skills automatically brings health of body and spirit.

Man now has knowledges and skills which enable him to control ever-enlarging areas of his experience. Man is capable of exercising power undreamed of a few years ago. But modern man also faces new frustrations and problems as he seeks to reassess his place in a vast cosmos, and as he wrestles with new problems attendant upon a technological culture. In the arena of his inner life, man must still deal with fears, anxieties, sorrows. He still asks, "What is the meaning of life? Is life worth living? What is the most enduring ground of hope?" These are essentially religious questions. It is reasonable to assume that man will continue to ask them. It is reasonable to assume that man will continue to seek a frame of reference for his living and understanding beyond the perceptible and measurable.

Religion and the Wonder of Being Human

If religion has functioned in bringing hope in the presence of the limiting and demoralizing experiences of life, it has also functioned in reference to man's strengths and possibilities. We have noted that a part of the wonder of human existence is the capacity for self-transcendence and situation-transcendence. The meaning of human life is not wholly determined by the pains and pleasures of the moment. Man lives in terms of memories and hopes, visions and values which transcend the immediate situation.

Historically, religion has functioned in providing a vision of reality which has brought challenge as well as consolation. In religious devotion men have righted wrongs, combated and overcome adverse circumstances, turned loss to gain, striven after ideals, assumed responsibility in the unending work of creation. Religion has brought a perspective of transcendence to bear upon the human situation. That perspective has put human efforts under judgment and called men to a life of growth into maturity. It has inspired man to seek worth in living which comes through creative effort, through realization of one's potentialities and through participation in "the sweep of the cosmos."

Deep in the heart of man are the dual urges for security and significance. Historically, religion has spoken to both. It provides a vision of that in which man may place his abiding trust. It also provides a vision of that toward which man can aspire. Religion is thus both consolation and challenge, reassurance and the call to adventure. A. H. Maslow, the psychologist, speaks of *deficit* and *growth* motives. Deficit motives seek reduction of tension. Growth motives maintain tension in the quest for unattained goals. The vision of God has brought to many a peace which passes understanding. It has also brought "a divine discontent" calling man to grow beyond what he is, to seek the ideal, to work for a better world.

As we look to the future, it seems reasonable to assume that man will continue to experience the needs for security and significance, for reassurance and challenge. Through science man will gain increasing control over nature. But in the midst of his increasing knowledge, skill, and power man will experience new frustrations, conflicts, and areas of mystery. In the midst of changing his external world, man will continue to experience the need for changes in himself. Such changes, both external and internal, will necessitate some guiding value-system and some faith as to what gives life its ultimate meaning. These are matters with which the sciences and arts deal only indirectly. These are matters to which religion has sought to speak more directly, representing its primary concern. Thus, Clyde Kluckhohn, the distinguished anthropologist, wrote:

> As wide an induction as anthropology can offer is that every society desperately needs morality in the sense of common standards, and religion in the sense of orientations toward such inescapable problems as death, individual responsibility, and other ultimate value attitudes. Religion in this sense is absolutely necessary to promote social solidarity and individual security by affirming and symbolically enacting a system of common purposes. In my opinion a faith is required which would not force intellectual reservation or conflict or compartmentalization.[2]

That man will continue to have needs for a basic orientation to existence in its wholeness appears to be the case. That much in traditional religion no longer speaks to many modern men also seems to be the case. The future of religion depends on whether there can be continuing progress toward a religion of maturity. Morale, in considerable measure, is a by-product of one's expectations and hopes. Insofar as God is a symbolic representation of the ground of man's ultimate hope, the doctrine of God (by whatever name it is called) will continue to be a matter of crucial concern to man. The need for continuing creative work in reference to the doctrine of God is obvious.

To be human is to live in an expanding universe not only physically but psychologically and emotionally. Present-day attempts to break through old molds and to communicate across lines of race, religion, nation, culture, and the present explorations into outer space exemplify man's urge to go beyond himself and to find fulfillment through participation in larger worlds of meaning. Unfortunately, religion has sometimes functioned in a restricting way. But it has also functioned in expanding ways, encouraging man in his curiosities and propensities for reaching out. The future of religion is bound up with the measure of imagination which can be brought to the religious quest. Creative imagination today calls for receptivity to new ways of seeing and thinking and feeling. We shall now look briefly at some contemporary ways of perceiving the universe and man. We shall then ask whether religion can incorporate such ways of seeing in the vision it seeks to communicate.

An Unfolding Universe

Contemporary knowledge enables us to see man as part of a cosmic spectacular. Man has come into being in relation to the evolutionary processes of the universe. He is not the darling of the universe, but he belongs. It is a universe favorable to growth in humanness, even though much pain is involved and there is no guarantee that all human desires will be satisfied.

Pierre Teilhard de Chardin, the distinguished paleontologist-priest, is only one of the contemporary writers inviting us to see the universe in more exciting ways.[3] He believed the universe is best understood as an unfolding whole. The model of static mechanism is not appropriate, for knowable reality is of the nature of process. Reality is dynamic, interrelated, attaining new levels of existence and organization. The processes of the universe are best understood, not simply in terms of origins but also in terms of directions and possibilities as well as of limitations.

In this processive universe man has arrived. Human life achieves significance in relationship to the trends of that universe insofar as they can be discovered; man must accept the evolutionary point of view. In man the seemingly diverse trends toward individuation and interrelation come together. In man the universe becomes conscious of itself, thinks and steers itself. Man is a creature with distinctive capacities for giving direction to life itself. He needs a philosophy which helps him achieve a "cosmic orientation"—a vision of himself in relation to the whole of being. Man's appropriate hope is not for escape from nature but for fulfillment in a dynamic, interrelated world which is ever advancing into the new.

Ours is an awesome universe, not only in its vastness and complexity, but in its evolutionary character and its openendedness. Such a universe does not promise safety or the satisfaction of all desires to its inhabitants, but it is potential for meaningful and hopeful living.

While contemporary thinkers disagree on many cosmological matters, there is an emerging consensus that the universe is most accurately perceived in dynamic, relational, and evolutionary terms. It is reasonable to assume that the life-cosmos orientation of modern man will increasingly reflect this way of understanding.

Man—A Creature of Possibility

Modern research reveals man also as a creature who can be best understood in dynamic, relational, and emergent terms. In this sense he shares the character of the universe of which he is a part.

Human nature is not a static, fixed substance. Rather, man is ever in process of becoming in relation to nature and other persons. No man is an island unto himself; he is in the world and the world is in him. By nature man is a creature molded in reciprocal relationships. He does not simply change within the world; he changes with the world. No person can be neatly located in one time and space; the reality of his being involves a matrix of relationships.

Studies of man and the universe do not justify a doctrine of inevitable progress. Neither do they support doctrines of the total depravity of man. Finite creature that he is, subject to frustration, conflict, and hostility, man engages in tragically destructive behavior. But he also has capacities for growth, cooperation, and nobility of life. Human nature is neither inherently evil nor inherently good. It is potential. In that potentiality lies hope. The same impulses which are involved in the most destructive behaviors of man are involved in the most creative behaviors of man. Hope for a better human future lies not in changing the fundamental drives, but in turning them to constructive channels.

It is instructive to hear from persons who have spent many years in the study of man in various cultures. By and large, there is hope in what we hear. Margaret Mead, the anthropologist, writes:

> I believe we have not even begun to tap human potentialities, and that by a continuing humble but persistent study of human behavior, we can learn consciously to create civilizations within which an increasing proportion of human beings will realize more of what they have it in them to be.[4]

Clyde Kluckhohn wrote:

> . . . perhaps the greatest lesson which anthropology can teach is that of the boundless plasticity of "human nature." . . . Man must humbly but with courage accept responsibility for the destiny of mankind . . . Man may be able to understand and control himself as much as he has demonstrably understood and controlled nonorganic nature and domestic animals. At least it is worth the trial.[5]

Gardner Murphy, for some years Director of Research at the Menninger Foundation, writes, "An attitude becoming a thoughtful, scientifically-oriented student of human nature is one of gratitude for the richness of its apparent possibilities. . . . because of man's capacity for intimate union with the stuff of this world . . . he may hope to do more than to transcend himself, may hope to become in each new emergent phase of his life a new kind of man."[6]

Modern educators recognize that the human creature has greater learning capacities *throughout the life span* than have been hitherto realized. The behavioral sciences are helping provide us with new insights into the creative potentialities of man. Such data as we have encourage us to think of human personality in dynamic rather than in static terms; in relational, rather than in isolative terms; in terms of becoming rather than in terms of being a fixed substance or nature. Gardner Murphy has gathered up a contemporary way of seeing human personality in these words: "Personality is considered here as a flowing continuum of organism-environment events."[7]

While this dynamic and relational way of perceiving man helps us see more clearly the nature of man's most persistent problems, it also helps us see his possibilities in a new light. Man need not be a helpless pawn in the face of external circumstances. He has capacities for coping with the threatening and sustaining aspects of his environment. His capacities for adaptation, cooperation, and growth are such that he may find increasing meanings in relation to a growing world. Perhaps most exciting of all is the fact that man has capacities for *going beyond himself* and becoming a new kind of man.

Thus, contemporary thinking about the universe and man encourages us to hope for a new man in a new age. The human creature continues to be his own biggest problem, but his self-understanding is increasing.

Religion in Evolutionary Perspective

If an evolutionary perspective is essential in understanding man and the universe, it is equally essential for an understanding of religion. Religion functions in various areas, in varying ways in different cultures. Its modes of functioning are profoundly influenced by growth in man's knowledges and skills. It has been so throughout the history of the human race, as man has sought a meaningful and hopeful relationship to the universe. It seems reasonable to assume that this will be the situation in the foreseeable future.

In its origins among primitive peoples, religion is magical. It functions in relation to man's struggle for survival and the satisfaction of basic needs.

On another level of human development, man recognizes the futility of imploring the gods for rain, good crops, good health, offspring, and so on. Man recognizes an orderliness in the course of events. He learns to distinguish more clearly what is within his control and what is beyond his control. He seeks the inner blessedness which comes from living in harmony with nature. He seeks serenity of spirit in the face of demoralizing aspects of life in the belief that there is a wisdom and goodness in the total scheme of things. The stoic way of life has much of resignation in it. The stoic settles for limited expectations. There is a measure of stoicism in all mature religion.

The religious life sometimes issues in a more positive attitude of joy and life-appreciation than is found in classic stoicism. William James speaks of religion making "easy and felicitous what in any case is necessary." This more positive, life-affirming attitude attends the conviction that life is a gift of God, or that God is present and at work in the environing world. Religion on this level is sometimes marked by a satisfying sense of the sustaining presence of God.

Historically, there has been still another manifestation of the religious spirit. In response to a challenging vision of God, man has aspired after some new goal or purpose recognized as having a claim upon him. The growth motive in man is encountered by what he believes to be the divine will or call or summons. Man commits himself in devotion to some self-transcending value or values. His religion now is not only a quest for security. It is an expression of a quest for significance in relation to what is central and enduring in the nature of things. It is response to an ultimate loyalty which transcends, judges, and illuminates loyalties to family, friends, community, work, nation.

Julian Huxley has expressed the opinion that twentieth-century man is less and less interested in a religion geared primarily to security. Contemporary knowledge and skills make available many things once sought through religious techniques. However, man does need and seeks a "consciousness of sanctity in existence" and a motivation for continuing development:

> Twentieth-century man, it is clear, needs a new organ for dealing with destiny, a new system of religious beliefs and attitudes adapted to the new situation in which his societies now have to exist. . . . Earlier religions and belief-systems were largely adaptations to cope with man's ignorance and fears. . . . But the need today is for a belief-system adapted to cope with his knowledge and his creative possibilities; and this implies the capacity to meet, inspire and guide change . . . the primary function of any system today must be to utilize all available knowledge in giving guidance and encouragement for the continuing adventure of human development.[8]

No one, of course, can predict with certainty what the future of religion will be in the modern world. However, in the light of past history and what we know of man, it seems reasonable to assume that there will be a continuing concern for finding the morale, meaning, and motivation which men have sought through the religions of the world.

That men shall find a faith, which in the words of Kluckhohn, does "not force intellectual reservation or conflict or compartmentalization" is devoutly to be wished. Such a faith must adopt dynamic, relational, and evolutionary views of man and the universe. To be religiously useful it must be faithful to the testimony of man's inner life, including the sense of the holy. It must present a doctrine of God which does not contradict such knowledge as we have, but which points to a dimension of ultimacy and wholeness with which science does not directly deal. Alfred North Whitehead expressed the heart of religious aspiration in these words:

> Religion is the vision of something which stands beyond, behind, and within the passing flux of immediate things;

> something which is real, and yet waiting to be realized; something which is a remote possibility, and yet the greatest of present facts; something that gives meaning to all that passes, and yet eludes apprehension; something whose possession is the final good, and yet is beyond all reach; something which is the ultimate idea, and the hopeless quest.[9]

The current search for a viable doctrine of God is inconclusive, often confusing, and yet essential. The traditional static and other-worldly categories in which theological ideas have been expressed are rapidly losing their meaning for modern man. It may be that we are on the threshold of asking the God-question and conceptualizing God in new ways. It may be that new forms of worship and new expressions of devotion will come into being. Of this we may be confident: As long as the urge for expression and fulfillment is a part of man, he will seek a meaningful and hopeful relationship with that ultimate reality or combination of realities from which life comes and in which human destiny is fulfilled.

5.
Major Obstacles to Belief in God

There lives more faith in honest doubt,
Believe me, than in half the creeds.

SO WROTE Tennyson. Honest doubt is a fact. There are persons who take the agnostic or atheist position because they feel they have no alternative. There are others who would like very much to affirm the reality of God, but they are haunted by serious questions and doubts. There are others who seem to believe and disbelieve at the same time.

Any book which presumes to affirm the reality of God must give due recognition to the major obstacles to belief in God. Any concept of God which is offered for serious consideration must take into account the major challenges to theistic belief. The fact that a mature religion might be desirable does not necessarily mean that it is possible. The fact that we use the word "God" does not prove that there is that in the nature of things to which the word God refers. It is our purpose in this chapter to consider some of the major obstacles to belief in God in our time.

Is Belief in God Just a Projection of Our Wishes?

C. E. M. Joad once wrote, "To say that there is a God is not to say anything more than that we need to think that there is, and the need is in no sense a guarantee of the existence of that which satisfied it."[1] It seems evident that a good deal of wishing often goes into our affirming of the reality of God. Belief in God seems to be desirable; thus, we are inclined to make the affirmation.

In *The Future of an Illusion* Sigmund Freud presented his famous argument to the effect that the strength of religious ideas is "due to the fact that they are the fulfillment of the most insistent wishes of man." The human creature finds himself in a harsh and threatening world. Functioning in terms of the pleasure principle, he seeks satisfaction for his desires, but frustration is a part of the human lot. Thus, man "projects" his wishes upon the environing reality. God is the image of the heavenly father "created by a continuation of the child's helplessness before his earthly father," affording reassurance in the presence of life's threatening aspects. Religion is thus interpreted as being infantile, wish-projecting, neurotic, and often satisfying, all at the same time.

As one looks into his own experience and endeavors to understand that of others, he may recognize the presence and operation of projecting mechanisms. Our wishes play an important role in our thinking and believing. We tend to believe what we want to believe. It is understandable that this should carry into the religious life. It is not surprising that human beings should sometimes create concepts of God which appear to make gods in the image of man.

Whether the projection of human wishes and fantasies upon divine objects automatically disproves the reality of God, or proves religion to be an illusion, is another question. There is no self-evident reason why we should think either the best or the worst of the universe or the human situation. We do well to recall that projection is a two-way matter. If belief in God is a projection of dependence and love associated with the earthly father, by the same token *atheism* may be interpreted as the projection of distrust and/or hatred associated with the male parent.

While the psychological mechanisms to which Freud and others point are highly significant, they are not finally determinative when we raise the question of the reality of God. There are other relevant considerations.

Are the Arguments for the Existence of God Really Valid?

Various attempts have been made to prove the existence of God as a Supreme Being, external to the world, yet relevant to it. Among the most famous of these are the cosmological, teleological, ontological, and moral arguments.

These arguments have been subjected to careful scrutiny. Interested readers may find an abundance of material dealing with the pros and cons of the arguments.[2]

The cosmological argument holds that from the existence of the world we may legitimately infer the existence of God as cause of the world. The teleological argument holds that from the design or purposiveness of the world we may legitimately infer a divine Designer. Both arguments assume the validity of the category of cause, and both rest on the assumption that there is a Being which exists through its own necessity or nature.

Both of these assumptions have been seriously challenged. The notion of "cause" has undergone major rethinking in modern times. We seldom think of a single cause of a complex phenomenon. Rather, for every effect there is a field of relational factors. That there is an external creator or designer which brought the world into being can neither be proved nor falsified, but the existence of such a creator is not a logical necessity. One may fairly ask, "Who or what created the creator?" With equal fairness one might ask, "If something must be self-sufficient and eternal, why should it not be the world-order as well as a creator behind the world order?"

The cosmological and teleological "proofs" are interesting attempts to establish the existence of God, but they are somewhat less than convincing save to those who are already convinced. In recent years the teleological argument has lost some of its force in the awareness that "design" or "purpose" is a category of limited applicability in man's inclusive environment. In the order of nature the ideas of design and directionality must be held in conjunction with the concept of randomness. Both seem to be present.

The ontological argument (developed by Anselm and Descartes) holds that the very idea of a supreme or perfect Being (God) implies his existence. If he did not exist, he would not be perfect or supreme, for existence is implicit in the idea of perfection. While this is a fascinating argument and has been presented with variations, it is evident that in calling God most real or most perfect we have simply *declared* God's existence, but have not proved it.

The philosopher Immanuel Kant examined the cosmological, teleological, and ontological arguments and found them wanting. He concluded that the existence or nonexistence of God cannot be proved on the basis of pure or theoretical reason. One is left in the agnostic position so long as he appeals only to reason of that kind. However, he insisted, there is also a practical or moral reason—and it is as a postulate of practical reason that we may affirm the reality of God. There are certain demands inherent in man's moral nature, according to Kant. Conscience assumes that the moral ideals are realizable but such realization is possible only if there is a supreme moral will (God). Thus, God is said to be a postulate of the moral law which is given in man and in the nature of things.

Kant himself apparently came to have some second thoughts about his own formulation of the moral argument. It carries with it a built-in presupposition that man's moral purposes and goals must be guaranteed fulfillment here or in the hereafter through the agency of a supreme moral will. This entails a major leap of faith. However, a number of philosophers in the Kantian tradition have been prepared to take that leap, insisting that God is disclosed in the moral imperative and in the influence it exerts upon us. Furthermore, it is argued that belief in God tends to strengthen and give sanction to moral behavior, and thus is justified on pragmatic grounds.

Some persons regard the arguments for the existence of God which we have been considering as valid arguments. Others regard them as logically invalid and meaningless. Still others regard them to be poor arguments, as arguments, but nevertheless significant in the theological concern which they reveal. Still others, who believe in God on grounds other than rational argument, find a measure of support and reassurance in these arguments. Thus, we see that there is no consensus on this matter.

It is significant that relatively few contemporary theologians appeal to the traditional theistic arguments as the primary basis for affirming the reality of God. Many theologians do not regard the arguments as being very convincing. Furthermore, even if one did accept the validity of the arguments, there is no assurance that the God whose existence was thereby proved would be the God of religious faith. The God in whom the theologian is interested is the God who is the ultimate ground of hope disclosed in man's experience of healing, redeeming grace. The traditional arguments for the existence of God do not necessarily lead to such a God. Thus, on several grounds serious questions are raised as to the significance of the various rational arguments for the existence of God as a Supreme Being transcendent to the world-order.

Some people believe that unless the existence of a supreme, transcendent, divine Being can be rationally proved, or demonstrated by something akin to scientific methodology, all talk of God is meaningless. Lacking such proof or verification, one is said to face an insuperable obstacle to belief in God. In response to such claims, there are those who insist that religious faith is not primarily grounded in rational argument; furthermore, to affirm the reality of God involves much more than giving intellectual assent to a particular concept of God. We shall have occasion to speak of these matters in later chapters.

Can the Reality of God Be Reconciled With Suffering and Tragedy?

Probably no single obstacle to belief in God looms larger in the thinking of many persons than the presence of seemingly unproductive suffering and tragedy in the world. How can one reconcile the reality of a God who is both powerful and good with the fact of such suffering and tragedy?

Many attempts have been made to resolve "the problem of evil," as it is sometimes called. Some have said that if man had God's perspective or view of all things, he would recognize that all seeming evil is really leading to some larger good, or is actually a part of a pattern which is good. Some have said that God *wills* only the good, but he is limited (1) by the free choices of human beings, (2) by some contrary evil force, (3) by something in his own nature which limits him, (4) by the structures of things within which he must work. Still others have suggested that God is both powerful and good, only God's goodness is different from man's limited views of goodness. Still others have said that the problem of evil transcends human understanding, but we are justified in "betting our lives" that God is bringing or will bring good out of man's deepest suffering and tragedy.

Some persons find these "solutions" to the problem of evil illuminating and helpful; others regard them as rationalizations. In either case, all human beings experience the pain of being human; any mature faith must give some kind of accounting of suffering and tragedy and some vision of hope in their presence.

There are those who believe that in order to maintain intellectual integrity in the presence of unproductive suffering, we must give up belief in a God who is both good and powerful enough to influence the course of events. Surely such a God would not, we are told, cause or permit the prolonged suffering which attends some terminal illnesses, the deterioration which sometimes attends the aging process, mishaps which bring major handicaps, invalidism, premature deaths, the loss of a mate or other person around whom much of life's meaning has revolved. Surely a God of power and goodness, we are told, would not permit or cause conditions whereby millions of persons die of starvation, suffer the consequences of ignorance, live under conditions of injustice and cruelty.

In the early years of life we all experience a primitive credulity, believing almost everything we are told. But in time we experience a collision of evidence with prior belief—and then the doubting process begins to work within us. Some of the most agonizing doubts which we experience attend the collision of experienced suffering and tragedy with previously held ideas about a God of goodness and of power. Whereas the experience of adversity leads some persons to a deeper faith, it turns others away from belief in the reality of God.

Alfred North Whitehead wrote, "All simplifications of religious dogma are shipwrecked upon the rock of the problem of evil."[3] A religion of maturity does not rest content with facile explanations or solutions. Rather, it endeavors to help man to see reality in its wholeness (including both good and evil) and to find the meaning of his life in relation to the whole of being. It does not promise security, but it does point to the goal of significance in living. In the presence of suffering and tragedy it does not offer simple explanations or give pious admonitions. Rather, it communicates the vision of God in the midst of the pain and wonder of being human. But "seeing God" cannot come at the cost of denying or evading stubborn facts. It may come at the price of sincere and painful probing as we seek a more adequate way of thinking and speaking of God. One of the acid tests of any doctrine of God is its capacity to illuminate the fact of evil, to communicate the reality of God in relation to it, and to point the way to a hopeful confrontation of it. In the absence of such a doctrine of God, many persons of integrity will choose the way of humanism.

Can the Worlds of Science and Religious Faith Be Reconciled?

The coming of the scientific age has raised questions of basic importance for religious faith and belief in the reality of God. The Bible was written long before modern science came to be known. The historic creeds, classic theological systems, long-treasured religious symbols and rituals all came out of prescientific periods. In many instances they make affirmations which appear to be incompatible with scientific views and understandings. Indeed, the question is often raised as to whether science does not discredit belief in God. There are those who are convinced that science represents a major obstacle to belief in God, at least in any traditional sense.

It is well to recognize that certain tensions inevitably exist between science and theology. This is because they are dealing with different kinds of problems, they use different methods, they work within somewhat different frames of reference, they speak different languages. For these reasons it is not easy to establish communication between the scientific and religious communities. Fortunately, much progress is being made in terms of clarifying the respective concerns, methods, worlds, and languages of religion and science. There is more communication going on.

However, we cannot deny that there are instances in which real conflict seems to occur. For example, if a theologian and a scientist offer contradictory explanations for the same fact (such as the appearance of human life on this planet), it is evident that we have a conflict situation. If the scientist and theologian proceed in terms of contradictory presuppositions (determinism over against some form of freedom), it is evident that conflict is present. If the theologian and scientist fail to define with care their respective fields of inquiry, there is the possibility that they will get into each other's areas. Fortunately, it is becoming clearer that science and religion are not competing disciplines. They have their distinctive interests and responsibilities. Modern man is not forced to choose between them.

Despite the gains which have been made in establishing communication between the religious and scientific communities, much confusion still remains. Many thoughtful persons wonder how God relates to or is relevant in the world as pictured by science.

At the heart of the confusion is the waning sense of supernaturalism in the contemporary world. Science seeks explanations within nature itself. There appears to be no place for divine intervention in the scientist's world. Man finds his way to truth through investigation and the testing of hypotheses, not through revelation or some infallible authority, be it book, person, or institution. In his book *Science and Religion,* Harold Schilling, a physicist, defines nature as "the whole economy or system of observable phenomena and things, including man, existing in time and space, and held together in a field or web of cause-effect relationships."[4] The scientist confines himself to the study of natural phenomena.

On the other hand, a great deal of religion in the past has presupposed a three-story universe and a supernatural realm independent of the field of cause-effect relationships in which man lives, moves, and has his being. God has been portrayed as "other-worldly," his relationship to the world has been regarded as one of miracle, and he has often been regarded as the outside first cause who started the natural process, sustains it, and will bring it to a fitting fulfillment. Many persons who have studied science have given up belief in a three-story universe, supernaturalism, and divine intervention in the traditional sense. They accept scientific explanations for natural phenomena, and when there is a human problem (be it in the area of human maladjustments, disorders, or group conflicts) they look within man, his relationships, and the natural world for answers. So amazing have been the achievements of science that some persons ask, "Of what relevance is God in the modern world?"

The situation is complicated by the fact that many churches continue to use forms of worship which are thoroughly traditional and supernaturalistic in their orientation. Attempts are sometimes made to give theological answers to what are really scientific questions. God is still interpreted in some circles primarily as the worker of miracles and the One whose name should be used to fill in the gaps in man's understanding. Not infrequently languages are used which seem to contradict man's contemporary understandings of an orderly and evolutionary universe. The thoughtful layman is often confused. Must he choose between the leadings of his reason and scientific inquiry, on the one hand, and the teachings of his faith, on the other?

Must the affirmation of God's reality come at the price of one's intellectual integrity?

Thus, the advent of modern science, with attendant new ways of understanding man and the universe, raise basic questions about God. One of the major tasks of theology is to clarify the issues and to define relevant terms. That is why the more serious theologians of our time are insisting that we try to clarify what we mean when we use the word "God." We need greater precision in formulating the God-question.

Are the Obstacles to Belief in God Insuperable?

We have been considering some of the persistent questions and challenges which are raised in reference to the reality of God and the role of religion in the modern world. Where do they lead us?

We must take these various challenges with the greatest seriousness. If religion does have a vital function in the life of our time, we must seek to define it. If God can and should be taken into account in our hoping and understanding, we should try to be as clear as possible in expressing that conviction and in setting forth our conception of God.

This means that we must be prepared to speak to the various challenges to faith. It will not do to evade them or minimize their importance. Thus, any doctrine of God worthy of serious consideration in our time must be clear in indicating how the word God is being used and to what it refers. If one affirms the reality of God he may fairly be asked on what grounds he makes the affirmation, and what the affirmation means. A vital religion in our time requires a doctrine of God which can make some kind of sense in the face of the various obstacles to belief which have been set forth in this chapter. Lacking such a doctrine of God, the future of religion is dim.

It is not the purpose of this book to argue that anyone ought to be religious or ought to believe in God. It is the purpose of this book to give some indication of the nature of religion and its role in human life. More specifically, it is our purpose to seek an understanding of the God-idea and then to ask if we can speak meaningfully of the reality of God. This discussion must proceed in the context of revolutionary currents of thought and in the presence of major challenges to religion as we have known it.

6.
Reformulating the God-Question

IT IS FREQUENTLY assumed that the central issue pertaining to God can be stated simply: "Does God exist?" From this flows a second question: "What is the nature of God?"

It is the purpose of this chapter to suggest that there may be a more fruitful way of asking the God-question. Affirming the reality of God may involve much more than giving our intellectual assent to the proposition that a certain kind of being exists. Possibly we are sometimes diverted from significant theological discoveries because we begin our inquiry at the wrong point, concentrating on something other than the crucial issues. We would do well to clarify, first of all, what it is we are proposing to talk about when we propose to talk about God.

The Question Behind the Question

Dr. John Macquarrie tells the story of giving a lecture in which he used the word "God." Following the lecture a scientist in the audience said, "The speaker was quite intelligible until he introduced the word 'God' into his talk. This word does not stand for anything within my range of concepts, or experience, and so every sentence in which it was used was to me meaningless. . . . Will the speaker kindly tell us what the word 'God' signifies?"

The scientist put his finger on a crucial issue. If we are to speak meaningfully about God, we must have some understanding of what it is we are talking about. If we propose to ask questions about the existence or nature of God, we must have some prior notion as to what the God-idea is. Indeed, until we have clarified what the God-idea is, we are not in a position to formulate the relevant questions.

It is interesting to observe how we often assume what the God-idea represents without really looking into the matter. For example, in the last chapter we considered some of the major "obstacles" to belief in God. Every one of those "obstacles" was based on some presupposition as to what it is we are talking about when we use the word "God." The traditional theistic arguments (cosmological, teleological, ontological, moral) all assume that when we talk about God we are referring to a Supreme Being, existing apart from the world although possibly having some continuing relation to it. But is that what the God-idea always means?

Some of the arguments to the effect that belief in God cannot be reconciled with suffering and tragedy presuppose that the word "God" refers to a reality who plans or causes suffering and tragedy—or in some sense is responsible for it. But does the God-idea necessarily mean that?

Persons who argue that belief in God and modern science cannot be reconciled bring certain presuppositions about the God-idea to their argument. They frequently assume that when we use the word "God" we are referring to a Being whose nature and whose ways of acting are contradictory to the ways of things as pictured by science. But is this necessarily the case?

It is evident that meaningful communication about God

presupposes some shared understanding of what it is we are proposing to talk about. We must clarify the question behind all specific questions about God. We are not in a position to debate the respective merits of various God-concepts until we have agreed on what it is that God-concepts have in common. What is the context of relevance in which all God-concepts belong? What is the arena in which God-talk can appropriately go on, and what are the ground rules?

Let us assume that we decide to have a discussion about God. I might say, "That is splendid. I have been wanting to have a good talk about chairs for a long time." You might reply, "No, we have decided to talk about God, not chairs." To which I might reply, "But when we are talking about chairs we *are* talking about God." In exasperation you might respond, "But that is foolish. God is not a chair or the sum total of all chairs. God is a different kind of reality. We have agreed to talk about *God*." To which I might appropriately reply, "Very well, but what kind of reality *is* God? How can we know when we are really in the area of God-talk and not chair-talk? When are we justified in naming something *God*? What is the God-idea?"

It is evident that much of the confusion which exists in contemporary discussion of God goes back to the fact that we have not asked the basic question: What is the meaning of the God-idea? Until we have faced that question we are not in a position to evaluate specific God-concepts, nor are we in a position to raise questions about the reality of God. Only after we have clarified the meaning of the God-idea can we ask, "Is there that in *reality* to which the God-idea refers?" Furthermore, in clarifying the meaning of the God-idea we pave the way for determining the appropriate data to be considered and the methods to be used in meaningful discussion of God. Just as a scientist must define his problem before he can seek the relevant evidence, so the theologian must clarify the meaning of the God-question before he can propose relevant answers to it.

Two Perspectives from Which the God-Question Is Asked

In *Alice In Wonderland* we read, "'When I use a word,' Humpty-Dumpty said, 'it means just what I choose it to mean—neither more nor less.'" It is evident that the word "God" has many different meanings for different people. Perhaps, with Humpty-Dumpty, we have the right to use that word as we choose. However, unless we can agree on some meanings for the word, we cannot understand each other. It may be helpful to note that the word has come to have different meanings in terms of the perspectives from which it is approached.

These are those who use the word "God" from the *perspective of intellectual curiosity*. One may ask, "Did the world have a beginning? If so, who or what brought it into being? What is the explanation for things being as they are? How can we account for specific events?" Not infrequently people have said, "God is the explanation for the world and for what goes on in it." Thus, the meaning of the God-idea is regarded as that of *an explanatory principle*.

Proceeding from this assumption, a specific concept of God as supernatural causal agent is sometimes set forth. The question then emerges, "Does God, so conceptualized, really exist?" The cosmological and teleological arguments are designed to speak to that question. From this perspective, the existence and nature of God as causal agent is regarded as being the crucial God-question.

However, we may approach talk of God from another perspective: *that of a living human being who is asking the crucial questions pertaining to his own existence and that of others to whom he is related*. In Chapter One we considered how we all experience the pain and wonder of being human. It is out of the pain and wonder of human existence that the questions of courage and meaning and wholeness emerge. Is there a courage to affirm and celebrate life which overcomes the motive of shrinking back? Is there the possibility of a meaningfulness in existence which overcomes the sense of emptiness and futility? Is there the possibility of a wholeness and fulfillment which overcomes the fragmentation, brokenness, and separation of so much of our existence? In the presence of the limiting restrictions within which we must live, is there an enduring ground of hope? The question of hope gathers together the questions of courage and meaning and wholeness.

We place our trust and find a measure of hope in many things: family and friends, business, community, worthwhile causes, the state. But we find that at best these bring us a limited hope. They can take us just so far. Then we run into limitations and demands with which they are not able to deal. In life and death we keep coming to and coming up against inexorable conditions which are there, bringing both life and death, frustration, and a measure of fulfillment. *Is there hope in the presence of the way things ultimately are?* Is there hope, not only in man's own strengths, his partial loves and loyalties, but in that which he continually keeps coming to and coming up against in life and death? This is the question of God when asked from the perspective of the human being who is asking the crucial questions pertaining to his own existence and that of others to whom he is related. This is the crucial *religious* way of formulating the question of God. It is the question of hope.

It is from this perspective that we shall be speaking in the rest of this book. In this framework of concern the God-idea refers to that in which men seek and find *trust and hope*, not only in the more usual events and experiences of life, but in the presence of the boundaries, limits, and basic conditions relating to our existence. The religious question leads us into some of the issues raised out of intellectual curiosity, but its focus is on the enduring ground of hope.

To speak of God, then, is to speak of the dimension of

ultimacy. The word ultimate suggests coming to or being at an end. The dimension of ultimacy suggests that which we are forever *coming to, encountering, coming up against* in life and death. It is the affirmation of religion that trust and hope are appropriate responses to the Ultimate. To speak the word "God" out of personal experience is to affirm the coming of courage, meaning, wholeness, and hope in the presence of the deepest pain and the profoundest wonder of being human. The God-idea is that of the Ultimate-Real-Other experienced as faith and hope conferring.

The Testimony of Those Who Hope

The question of God rises out of life itself. We cannot escape the experiences, conditions, and issues which raise the question of an ultimate hope. To be sure, not all persons ask the question in theological language. Indeed, not all persons realize that they have theological concerns. But we all do have concerns which sometimes come to theological expression, and lie at the heart of theological inquiry.

Just as life is offered to persons on different terms, so life comes to have different meanings for various persons. Men give varying answers to the God-question. Just as the whole person asks the question of God, so the whole person gives answer. He gives answer not simply with beliefs he affirms, but in the character of his responding to the experience of being alive. He gives answer in his attitudes, commitments, actions. For some persons it is an answer of distrust, boredom, shrinking back, or even despair. For them life seems to hold only fleeting meanings at best.

For others, there is more of the religious response of hope rooted in trust. Life is not merely to be endured but to be celebrated. We do well to listen to the testimony of those who have come to some vision of God and in that vision have found trust and hope.

Job is portrayed as saying, "Though he slay me, yet will I trust in him" (JOB 13:15 KJV). Paul affirmed, "None of us lives to himself, and none of us dies to himself. If we live, we live to the Lord, and if we die, we die to the Lord; so then, whether we live or whether we die, we are the Lord's" (ROMANS 14:7-8). Undergirded by that trust he went on to say, "May the God of hope fill you with all joy and peace in believing, so that by the power of the Holy Spirit you may abound in hope" (ROMANS 15:13). In our own time there are many persons, some of whom we probably know, who bear witness to a life of hope rooted in trust. From his Nazi prison cell Dietrich Bonhoeffer wrote of his ambivalent thoughts and feelings, with weakness and strength, fear and faith so strangely intermingled. At the same time he could affirm the reality of his relationship with God:

> *Who am I? They mock me, these lonely questions of mine.*
> *Whoever I am, Thou knowest, O God, I am thine!*[1]

Hope and trust may be present in the midst of intellectual uncertainty and low tides of the spirit. They also bring the note of expectancy and life-affirmation to the coming of each day.

It is a fact that some persons attach confidence to and find hope in the mysterious reality by virtue of which we come into being, are what we are, and pass away. The coming of the life of faith and hope is not easily explained, although we do have some understanding of it. The person of faith seldom thinks of it as an achievement of his own. Rather, to such a person the life of faith and hope comes at the meeting point of man's search for God and God's coming to man. In this sense, hope, rooted in faith, is a gift.

There are striking similarities in the testimonies of those who speak of God's coming to man: The sense of the holy or awesome, the sense of one's own finitude in the presence of the divine, the experience of a healing-saving grace, the experience of being called to make God's cause one's own cause. Specific events or persons are said to mediate the vision of God and to elicit the response of faith and hope and commitment. This is the meaning of revelation.

Thus, in the experience of the person of faith and hope, the primary question of God is answered. He is convinced of the reality of God as the ground of enduring hope. Other questions appear in the light of the vision of God: How can I speak of the God whose light has come upon me? How can I communicate to others what God has come to mean to me? How can I live out the vision which has come and be faithful to it? These are the questions of the person who affirms the reality of God. He is not relieved of intellectual striving, moral struggle, or the basic pains of being human. But all these things, and all life, are given a changed meaning in the light of the vision by which he lives, and the hope in which he walks.

The Continuing Task of Theology

This chapter has issued in the proposition that the God-idea is the idea of an ultimate, objective ground of faith and hope. With this understanding the crucial God-question becomes: In what sense, if any, can we meaningfully affirm that there is that in or about reality which corresponds to the God-idea? Are faith and hope appropriate responses to life in its wholeness, or must man project fictional worlds, or seriously limit his frame of orientation, in order to sustain his spirit? Is man alone in the universe or not?

It is the continuing task of theology to wrestle with the God-question by drawing on the wisdom of the past, on man's varied experiences, on the testimony of historic communities of faith, on all available knowledge—utilizing the tools of critical analysis and constructive thought. It is the continuing task of theology to reflect on the life of faith, systematically setting forth its intellectual content. It is the continuing task of theology to give intellectual expression to man's unfolding perceptions of new revelations of truth. Thus, theology has conserving, evaluating, and constructing functions, helping man to move ahead in his quest for a clearer vision of God and a more mature faith.

In the next section we shall consider some of the issues bearing on a contemporary way of approaching the God-question. We shall look at some of the ways in which the reality of God is being affirmed by contemporary theologians. We shall ask: How can we speak of the vision of God in a way which is faithful both to the knowledge we have and to the claims of the religious life?

AFFIRMING THE REALITY OF GOD

Part Two

7.

An Appropriate Agnosticism

THE MINISTER was reading the words of the Ninetieth Psalm:

Lord, thou hast been our dwelling place
in all generations.
Before the mountains were brought forth,
or ever thou hadst formed the earth and the world,
from everlasting to everlasting
thou art God.

(PSALMS 90:1-2)

As these words were being read, the congregation was startled by a loud noise. A plane had broken the sound barrier.

In what way can the reality of God be affirmed in an age when man can travel faster than the speed of sound and make decisions which once were assumed to be God's alone? The Psalmist spoke in a prescientific age; what would he say now? He who would affirm the reality of God in the twentieth century must take into account many factors the Psalmist knew nothing about.

Our contemporary situation is not only that of knowing and being able to do so much. It is also that of discovering how little we know about many matters. Education has been defined as the process of becoming increasingly aware of one's ignorance. There are many areas in which the wise person says, "We do not know." The person of integrity does not claim to know more than he really knows.

It is the purpose of this chapter to suggest that there is an appropriate agnosticism in dealing with religious issues. Indeed, he who has never experienced doubt nor been baffled by mystery cannot affirm the reality of God in a mature way. To affirm the reality of God does not imply that one thinks he has all the answers. Recognition of mystery and the affirmation of the reality of God go hand in hand. To acknowledge this is to raise two questions: (1) Can the life of faith and "an appropriate agnosticism" actually coexist? (2) If so, how is it possible to entertain an "appropriate agnosticism" and affirm the reality of God at the same time? What can we say about God while acknowledging that there is much we do not know?

The Hiddenness of God

In approaching these matters, it is well to recall that in the Judeo-Christian tradition the reality of God and the hiddenness of God have been affirmed at the same time.

In Isaiah 45:15, we read, "Truly, thou art a God who hidest thyself." The Psalms affirm that the heavens declare the glory of God, but they also express the pain of feeling God's absence: "How long wilt thou hide thy face from me? How long must I bear pain in my soul and have sorrow in my heart all the day?" (PSALMS 13:1-2). "Why dost thou stand afar off, O Lord? Why dost thou hide thyself in times of trouble?" (PSALMS 10:1). "My God, my God, why hast thou forsaken me?" (PSALMS 22:1). Job asked, "Can you find out the deep things of God?" (JOB 11:7) and then cried out, "Oh, that I knew where I might find him, that I might come even to his seat!" (JOB 23:3). In writing to the Corinthians, Paul affirmed the reality of God but also spoke of man's limited knowledge, saying, "For now we see in a mirror dimly . . ." (I CORINTHIANS 13:12).

In Biblical thought, God's hiddenness is affirmed along with belief in God's self-disclosure. God is known only where and when he chooses to reveal himself. Even in his revelation he does not explain himself: "Neither are your ways my ways, says the Lord. For as the heavens are higher than the earth, so are my ways higher than your ways and my thoughts than your thoughts" (ISAIAH 55:8-9). "How unsearchable are his judgments and how inscrutable his ways!" (ROMANS 11:33).

Through the centuries of Christian history many persons have affirmed the reality of God and the hiddenness of God at the same time. Augustine, for example, wrote, "Thou hast formed us for thyself, and our hearts are restless till they find rest in Thee." It was this same Augustine who said, "If you have been able to understand it, it is not God that you contemplate."

The doctrine of the Trinity affirms both the reality of God and the hiddenness of God, for just as a mask *(persona)* defines a role, it also serves to conceal. Luther, who witnessed to the grace of God in his own life, also spoke of God as "in His entirety incomprehensible and inaccessible to human reason. . . ." Pascal said, "Every religion which does not affirm that God is hidden, is not true." In the sixteenth century John of the Cross wrote of "The Dark Night of the Soul," witnessing to the spiritual desolation of one who having seen the vision of God now experiences the fading of the vision.

A number of contemporary theologians have stressed the doctrine of *Deus Absconditus*. In making the point that we cannot conceive but only acknowledge God, Karl Barth wrote, "We ought to speak of God. We are human, however, so we cannot speak of God. We ought, therefore, to recognize both our obligation and our inability, and by that very recognition, give God the glory."[1] Carl Michalson wrote, "The doctrine that God is hidden is probably the most pertinent Christian witness about God for our time."[2]

The persons who have been quoted have believed that there is much we do not know about God and that there are occasions when one experiences the seeming absence of God. Yet, it would not be accurate to refer to them as agnostic in the sense of holding that we can know nothing of God. In varied ways they have held together the convictions of God's reality and his hiddenness.[3] Thus, there are those who hold that the life of faith can and does coexist with a certain kind of agnosticism, but an agnosticism relieved by awareness of God's self-disclosure.

Living With the Fact of Mystery

Though some persons believe that a doctrine of the hiddenness of God is compatible with a doctrine of divine presence, there are others who find it difficult or impossible to make any affirmation about God because there is so much man cannot know about himself and the universe.

In his fascinating book *Of Stars and Men,* Harlow Shapley presents an astronomer's view of the universe. He points out that we have come far in the accumulation of verifiable facts. We have penetrated many of the secrets of the universe. At the same time, we have come to a growing awareness of the vastness and complexity of the universe. There is much we do not know. We are limited in the instruments which are available for probing into the mysteries of the physical universe.

Thus, Shapley combines a sense of mystery with a sense of wonder in man's situation:

> The new knowledge from many sources . . . makes obsolete many of the earlier world views. The new discoveries and developments contribute to the unfolding of a magnificent universe; to be a participant is in itself a glory . . . we are associated in an existence and an evolution that inspires respect and deep reverence. We cannot escape humility. And as groping philosophers and scientists we are thankful for the mysteries that still lie beyond our grasp.[4]

With the astronomer we may indeed feel a sense of awe and humility. But inevitably there comes the awareness that our knowledge is fragmentary. There are many unanswered questions about the origin of the solar system in which we live. There are unanswered questions as to the beginning of the universe, if it had a beginning. We may discern varied structures and processes, but our knowledge is partial. To speak of "the design of the whole" is speculative.

If much mystery attends the physical aspects of the universe and man, what shall we say when we move into a consideration of values and goals as they relate to man's decisions? Man's search for a meaningful and hopeful existence must be carried on in a universe which he comprehends only in limited measure.

The extent of man's ignorance poses a major problem as he confronts the God-question. Obviously, a certain reticence is appropriate in speaking of ultimate matters. If there be a God of truth, he is not honored by intemperate claims to knowledge of him. But even as we acknowledge all this, the haunting questions remain: If we cannot speak with finality about God, what meaning do God-statements have? Is it possible to live a meaningful, intellectually respectable life of faith while acknowledging the extensiveness of our ignorance? The agnostic thinks that silence in reference to ultimate matters is the part of wisdom. The man of faith insists the issue is not so simple as the agnostic would make it out to be. There are forced options in life. One must act *as if* certain things were true. One must often proceed to make choices and decisions even though he lacks all the relevant information.

Must One Be Half-Hearted if Only Half-Sure?

In writing of the nature of faith Gordon Allport has said, "One can be half-sure without being half-hearted. . . . Though it is not within our power to discern certain knowledge we do well to act decisively on the basis of whatever probability attends the object of our faith."[5]

The life of faith is not a life of having all the answers. It is a way of life-affirmation in response to the vision of God—even though that vision sometimes raises as many questions as it answers. Indeed, it appears that God is sometimes experienced, not so much as an answer, but as the hardest question one has ever encountered. We have come to a time when it is unrealistic to expect absolute certainty in theological matters. There are some things we can know with considerable assurance. We need to be faithful to such information as we have. We need to seek out realistic grounds of hope. But we must also make our mental peace with the necessity of living with many unanswered questions.

Dean Willard Sperry observed that profound religion is often more of an attitude than an answer. Referring to the Twenty-third Psalm, he suggested that this is a profoundly religious statement, not because it gives answers to the problems of death, but because it affirms an abiding trust and hope in the presence of death. To speak the name "God" is not necessarily to explain something or to give information. It may be to affirm confidence and indicate the direction of one's aspiring and hoping.

There is something to be said for the point that the demand for finality of knowledge (or claim to it) may reflect lack of faith rather than possession of it. Deep trust in any relationship does not demand a blueprint of the future or a contract in which all matters pertaining to the future are spelled out.

Belief is extremely important in the life of faith, but it is not the whole of the life of faith. Furthermore, belief itself is not simply a matter of having all the information one might wish. A belief, as Ralph Barton Perry pointed out, is an idea on which we are prepared to act. On his eightieth birthday E. Stanley Jones said, "I don't know what the future holds, but I do know who holds the future." He was expressing a faith-attitude which gathered up belief, an appropriate agnosticism, and an affirmation of the venture of life.

Some Pitfalls to Be Avoided in Speaking of God

To acknowledge that man lacks important information in many areas is to sound a warning to persons who propose to speak of the reality of God. As has been said, a certain reticence is appropriate. There are pitfalls to be avoided.

It has long been a temptation for theologians and others to insert the word "God" into the empty spaces of man's knowledge. However, there is no reason to believe that being "religious" gives one access to information withheld from scientists and others—religious or not. It is not the function of theology to compete with various intellectual disciplines including the sciences. Theology and science deal with the same world but they ask different questions, employ different methods, and have distinctive vocabularies.

The fact of mystery is a warning against dogmatism in theological as well as in scientific matters. The dogmatic stance is increasingly untenable in a world of increasing knowledge and increasing awareness of what we do not know. There is much evidence indicating that the life of mature faith does not require the belief that one has achieved finality of knowledge in theological matters.

The awareness that there are many matters of which we cannot speak with assurance raises important questions as to how statements about God are meaningful. For example, the question might be raised as to whether it is possible to know very much about the nature of God, as such. It is well to recall that many responsible theological thinkers have insisted that we may speak of the acts of God, how and where God is experienced, God's disposition toward man, the meaning of God in human experience—but that knowledge of the nature or inner reality of God eludes human beings.

In one of his sermons Martin Luther said, ". . . no human wisdom has been able to conceive what God is in himself, or in his internal essence. Neither can anyone know or give information of it except it be revealed to him by the Holy Spirit." If within the community of faith one finds that kind of reservation in speaking of God, we do well to exercise care in asserting how statements about God are meaningful.

What, then, can be said of an affirmative character? If affirming the reality of God does not fill the gaps in scientific knowledge, or provide final answers in theological-ethical considerations, or tell us all we would like to know about the nature of God, what meaning can attend our speaking of God? What does it mean to affirm the reality of God and in what way or ways does speech concerning God bear on the question of hope? What sort of hope is appropriate in the face of the mysteries which envelop us? How does our speech about God articulate that hope and give direction to it?

In the past we have often assumed that statements about God are usually informative statements, telling us certain facts about God and how things are. It has been assumed that the most relevant way to speak of God is to speak of the existence and nature of God. In recent years, however, a great deal of attention has been given to theological language and the way it functions in our lives. We are beginning to see that theological language (including speech about God) has varied meanings of great importance. The study of language is opening new dimensions in theological studies. Out of the discussion of how *not* to talk about God new insights are emerging as to how we may speak meaningfully of the reality of God. We turn next, then, to a consideration of theological language. In the process we may come to see more clearly what we are really saying and doing when we affirm the reality of God.

8.
The Strange and Varied Languages of Faith

TO BE HUMAN is to be in communication. Selfhood emerges in relationships where creative interchange is going on. To man it is given to communicate in varied languages, including verbal languages. By way of language we express our deepest feelings and highest hopes; we give utterance to our thoughts; we give of ourselves to others and receive from them; we open our lives to the world about us; through language we become more alive, more sensitive, more whole.

But language also has its restricting side. There are language barriers. If our vocabulary is limited, our words may fail to communicate our thoughts and feelings and aspirations. Sometimes language creates distorted images and leads to misunderstanding. Sometimes language actually blocks communication and we are confined by our limited vocabularies.

We have all been in groups where the conversation was deadening. Nothing of importance or excitement was being expressed. No one articulated anything with clarity. There was no creative interchange of thought and feeling. There were monologues of likes and dislikes. Words were used as an escape from silence.

We have been in groups of quite a different character. There was gracious and intelligent communication. One caught an excitement and wonder about life, a sensitivity in relationships. The words which were used communicated the feeling that life has range.

Thus, from experience we know about the restricting and expanding functions of language. Perhaps we have noticed that there is a connection between the quality of one's functioning as a human being and his communicative habits and skills. We become more human in communication. Through language we enter larger worlds of meaning. Through language we are made more aware of our world and are enabled to participate in deepened relationships within it.

In recent years increasing attention has been given to the role of language in the life of faith. Here, again, we discover the restricting and expanding functions of language. There is the language of limited perspective, dogmatism, demand for conformity, impoverishment of thought and feeling. On the other hand, the religious life is sometimes expressed in languages of wonder, awe, illumination, reverence, hope, and glad commitment. The languages of faith can be disruptive or uniting; they can encourage shrinking back or moving forward.

Growth toward maturity in religion involves growth in adequacy of expression. Many persons are fixated on a level of religious immaturity because of an impoverishment of linguistic tools. In moving out of childhood they have acquired no new words or images or symbols to express and communicate a growing faith. One of the major problems bearing on the spiritual life of man is that of finding more adequate languages of faith. If we are to affirm the reality of God meaningfully in our time, we must probe the varied and sometimes strange languages which attend the life of religion. We must seek a language appropriate to the greatness of our theme in order to communicate.

Language About Faith and the Languages of Faith

In Chapter Three we distinguished the observer's view of religion and the insider's view of the life of faith. This distinction is important as we consider the matter of language. There is a language *about* religion and there are the languages *of* religion. The observer may say, "Religion at its best inspires trust in God." The insider or participant may affirm, "The Lord is my shepherd, I shall not want." There is the language of description and analysis; there is the language of personal confession. They are different.

The language of personal confession is often confusing to the observer. The person of faith is likely to use words that sound "odd" or "strange" in the sense that they do not belong in the usual vocabularies of the secular world. One hears of God, grace, sin, redemption, salvation. The observer may well say, "Somehow I cannot locate these words on the map of my experience. They seem to be meaningless terms."

The person of faith may participate in rituals which to him are deeply significant. Through them values are celebrated and meanings communicated; but to the observer they may appear to be without point. The person of faith may be deeply moved by song and story related to his religious tradition; to the observer all this may have no relevance at all.

In previous chapters we have suggested that the word "God" is best understood within the vocabulary of religion. To be sure, a philosopher may choose to use the word "God" in relation to a cosmology or world-view he develops. Alfred North Whitehead and others have so used it. Normally, however, we think of the word "God" as a word having its primary relevance in the context of the religious life or the life of faith (for present purposes we are using those terms interchangeably). Thus, if we are to ask what it means to affirm the reality of God, we do well to ask, "What does it mean when the person of faith speaks of God and/or affirms the reality of God?" What is really going on and what is really being said and meant when the word "God" is used in religious discourse?

The upshot of this discussion thus far is twofold: (a) growth toward religious maturity involves the acquisition of more adequate linguistic tools and symbols; (b) an understanding of the distinctive languages of faith requires an understanding of how they are meaningful to the person of faith. One never understands the full theological significance of such terms as God and grace and sin and salvation simply by looking them up in the dictionary. They have something to do with the experience of the individuals using them. One needs to listen to the person of faith.

With this background, let us now consider some ways in which religious discourse functions within the life of faith.

What Religious Language Says and Does

For our present purposes we are using the term "language" to include systems of vocal and visual signs for the expression and communication of meaning. Signs point toward that to which attention is being directed. Symbols combine signs and agreed-upon meanings. Religious language, so understood, includes not only spoken and written words, but rituals, art, and other vehicles for the expression and communication of meaning.

In recent years it has been asserted by some thinkers that statements about God are meaningless. It is held that all cognitively meaningful language is either definitional or empirical in nature; religious language is neither definitional nor empirical in nature; therefore, no religious language is cognitively meaningful. There are those who go on to say that the existence of God can neither be verified nor falsified. Furthermore, it is characteristic of believers in God to affirm that belief in God is consistent with any possible state of affairs. Under these circumstances, it is held, nothing really meaningful is being said when the reality of God is affirmed. Apparently convinced by this line of thought, Paul Van Buren has written a book, *The Secular Meaning of the Gospel.* He addresses himself to the question, "How may a Christian who is himself a secular man understand the Gospel in a secular way?"[1] He goes on to say that the empirically minded, secular believer "does not know what to do with Theology. . . . Analogical as well as literal language about God makes no sense to him."[2] Thus, Van Buren proposes a Christological interpretation of the secular meaning of the gospel without reference to God.

How fruitful the current discussion of language will be for theology remains to be seen. However, out of the debates over the cognitive meaningfulness of statements about God there has emerged growing attention to the varied ways in which theological discourse functions in the lives of persons of faith. In speaking of God, the religious person may intend to make statements of fact—giving information about God, describing God, reporting how things are. It is the meaningfulness of such statements which has particularly been called into question by some who practice linguistic analysis.

Yet, it is clear that religious language is used in other ways as well. Much theological discourse performs a dual role—pointing toward that which is regarded as the Ultimate-Real-Other, *and* expressing the meaning of God in the experience of the person of faith. Thus, there is both an objective and a subjective reference in theological talk. To affirm "God is a faithful God" presumably is an attempt to say something about God and also to say something about one's experience of God.

Let us note briefly some of the ways in which religious discourse functions. It may serve to *express* given feelings, evaluations, aspirations in response to the vision of the divine. It may *evoke* responses of faith, trust, zeal, commitment, aspiration. It may *commend* given courses of action. It may *nurture* given life styles. Religious discourse may serve to *deepen bonds of communication and fellowship* within a community of faith. Thus, language is an integral part of the religious life, functioning in a variety of ways. It expresses and communicates the thoughts, feelings, and aspirations of men as they apprehend themselves in relation to the divine.

Religious symbols involve both concepts and images. Concepts are the tools of the theologian as he reflects on the faith and endeavors to express its content clearly and coherently. Concepts are fundamental in articulating a comprehensive belief system binding fact, value, and ultimate reality. Conceptual language is normally regarded as having some objective referent, pointing to a reality or realities other than man's thoughts, feelings, aspirations. Intellectual belief, as a phase of the life of faith, is expressed conceptually. Concepts (as of God) tend to be general, abstract, and expressed in definitional form.

The language of faith also involves much of imagery. The imagery of faith reflects the vision of God shared in a community of faith. The language of imagery includes sacred stories and dramas, pictures, parables, metaphors, analogies, models. Varied forms of imagery may be gathered up in the ritual, mythology, art, and literature of a people.

The imagery of faith functions in a variety of ways. It may express a basic attitude toward the world (a "blik," as R. M. Hare puts it). It may kindle awareness of qualitative dimensions of reality. It may point to fundamental human experiences now seen in a frame of orientation and devotion. It may direct attention to the interrelatedness of things, suggesting an ultimate unity. It may suggest a patternfulness in reality in relation to which man may come to recognize himself and achieve a sense of identity. Religious images may nurture life styles.

Some persons who have difficulty handling abstract ideas or concepts can identify with a picture, a story, or a drama. Indeed, for some people the images become a kind of theology. The picture, story, drama, or model provides a way of perceiving the life process in its ultimate context. Values, purposes, directions, goals are recognized and celebrated with the aid of such images. We speak of God in both concepts and images.

Thus, much is said with many different meanings in the varied languages of the life of faith. Theological terms, doctrines, whole systems of thought, rituals rich in imagery, scriptures employing varied modes of expression, all point in two directions: to the Ultimate-Real-Other and to the experiencing human being or fellowship of faith. It says something about each, but what it says is not always immediately apparent.

Theological languages are expressive of the whole person. Insofar as religions are total ways of life—involving knowledge, emotion, and action—it is essential that there should be various languages of faith, making various affirmations, expressing different meanings in varying contexts, expressing the divergent aspects of the life of faith. This is precisely what we find to be the case. But the widespread failure to grasp this point often gets us into serious trouble. We do not hear what is really being said. We cannot get along without the strange languages of religion—but neither can we get along with them!

The Perils of Religious Language

Having noted the crucial role of language in the life of faith, let us now give attention to the perils of religious language.

There are two kinds of perils to be guarded against. The first has to do with the claims which are made for religious statements. There is the peril of claiming too much or too little or what is inappropriate for what is expressed.

Persons speaking of religious matters run the risk of claiming to know more than they really know. The view that faith provides the answers sometimes leads to the conclusion that unless one claims to have all the answers he is not in a state of faith. It is difficult for many persons to understand that faith is trust and commitment as well as intellectual belief. It is not always easy to acknowledge that mature faith includes what we have described as an appropriate agnosticism.

A particularly dangerous temptation in religious discourse is to take a statement of limited applicability and stretch its claims to relevance beyond appropriate limits. The peril of overgeneralization is real. In this connection there are perils in the use of analogy in theological discourse. An analogy has limited applicability and cannot legitimately be used to justify statements as to how things are in a final and ultimate sense. Analogies are analogies, sometimes useful in suggesting hypotheses or ways of seeing things. But they are not arguments, nor do they constitute empirical evidence. For example, it is sometimes said that nature exhibits machinelike characteristics and therefore reality must be a vast machine. There is no doubt that the analogy has some validity, but it does not follow that reality in its wholeness can best be understood in mechanistic terms. There is much in reality also which suggests the analogy of an organism.

There is another, seldom recognized peril in religious discourse—that of saying too little. The religious person who affirms that God is good or omnipotent or personal, but then goes on to say that of course God is so different from human creatures that these adjectives are really unfathomable, is not saying very much. Certainly he is saying too little to be significant. In sophisticated ways we are sometimes given statements about God, presumably informative, but then told that the truths of God are beyond reason. An interesting question of integrity thus is raised when we are asked to assent to the truth of statements the meanings of which are said not to be comprehensible.

Another peril attendant upon language is related to the varied functions of religious discourse—informative, emotive, expressive, evocative, and so on. One may easily get language roles confused. For example, the language of worship and ritual may involve much of poetry, myth, drama. To insist that statements of objective fact are being made may be to miss the point.

In seeking the meaning of religious language it is essential that we try to understand the *intent* of what is said as well as the actual *content*. It is possible to take a language seriously without necessarily taking it literally. To insist on a literal reading of much religious literature may cause one to miss the real intention of it.

It is dangerous to assume that for every idea or every insight there is an exact word or an appropriate symbol. There is an ultimate loneliness of the mind and spirit. And so we use the linguistic tools which are available, knowing they are inadequate. It is likely that we have neither words nor syntax for the most important truths about the world and human life.

In addition to the claims made for it, there is a second kind of peril in religious language—that of failing to recognize the dynamic and contextual character of meaningful discourse. Words in themselves normally mean nothing. Meanings go back to persons, relationships, situations, experiences. There is an old homiletical adage to the effect that a text out of context is pretext. So it is with words and other symbols. They shift meanings; their functioning is in the context of dynamic events and relationships.

Affirmations of faith normally come out of experiences involving struggle, searching, illumination, and sometimes conflict. The words used have had some communicative significance in the original setting. The affirmation of faith probably fulfilled pointing, expressing, and evoking functions in its originating context. But this is no guarantee that the same affirmation of faith will have the same meaning if transplanted into another situation. The historic creeds all played significant roles in their origins. Today, lacking insightful interpretation, they may be the source of confusion.

Man is forever moving into new situations, experiencing new visions and values, asking new questions. Unless he has a language which is relevant where he is, expressive and communicative in the pain and wonder of his immediate life, he will be something less than human.

One of the tragedies of much church life today is the failure to speak a language that communicates, or to provide meaningful interpretation of traditional symbols. Simply speaking ancient words more loudly or setting them to new music does not make them more intelligible. Paul Tillich wrote, ". . . the traditional symbols of religion and concepts of theology are empty for those who do not experience them as answers to their questions."[3] One of the primary functions of the church is to initiate persons into the living languages of living faith. This is no simple task, but it is essential if we are to move toward religious maturity in a new age.

The Need for a Contemporary Language of Depth and Hope

Is it not strange that in the midst of affluence, life for so many persons can be so empty? That in the midst of a knowledge explosion, so many miss the wisdom of living sensitively, creatively, lovingly? That in the midst of people, individuals so often feel lonely and alienated? That in a time when men know the earth is not really flat, their inner world should become more flat? That in a time when every day brings forth new wonders, so many lose their sense of wonder and of hope?

Yet, something like this seems to be the case. Of course, many persons are living profoundly meaningful lives. But for vast numbers of human creatures the depth dimension of life is missing. Lacking an inner life, they become preoccupied with feverish activity or simply being entertained. This phenomenon is attended by the loss of meaning in distinctively religious language.

Dean Samuel Miller has written:

> A new way of looking at life, and therefore a new way of living and understanding things, has developed. . . . Something is missing. . . . The pageantry of myth and holy day, of poetry and ritual, has been swept away with a brusque, businesslike gesture, leaving all days alike, dulled down to a bitter frenzy of routine. The great metaphors have drooped and died. . . . In man's life everything has been denuded of its religious quality. Birth, puberty, marriage, sin, death—once the pivotal points of spiritual significance, have now lost their sacramental depth. Everything has become quite natural, biological, social, and quite clinical. There are no distances, no depths, no essential mysteries. Everything is on the surface, from which data can easily be skimmed off.[4]

Many of the great religious symbols of another day have lost their gripping and compelling power. Missing in our culture are new, vital symbols suggesting the dimension of transcendence, not in a supernatural or otherworldly sense, but in the sense of suggesting values and meanings "not realized in the immediate situation." If it be true that "an individual's self-image is built up out of symbols" as Rollo May suggests, it is obvious that our very destiny as human creatures is at stake. Clods and cogs need no vision of greatness symbolically expressed, but human beings do. It is as man recognizes himself in relation to some pattern or structure or vision of meaning that he grows in the finest human qualities. Hope is the flower of that vision, and self-understanding grows from it. Unfortunately, the most compelling symbols in our contemporary culture neither reflect nor nurture a vision of greatness or wholeness. Our impoverishment of speech in matters of ultimate concern is a symptom of our spiritual emptiness. Man becomes human in communication, but we seem to be able to communicate only about *things*. And in the process man himself becomes *a thing*. We need a contemporary language of depth and hope.

Can There Be a New Vision and Language of God?

In the past, the word "God" has been the major verbal symbol expressing man's vision of the transcendent dimension of existence and reality. To speak of God was not simply to speak of "a being out there." It was to speak of a way of seeing life as profoundly important and precious and of eternal significance. It was to speak of life as a gift and each day as a summons into living faith and devotion. It need hardly be said that multitudes of persons have attached great significance to the word God. To believe in God has made all the difference in their lives.

But today many persons are having trouble with the word because of its association with a certain world view. Traditionally God has been associated with a supernatural realm. For those holding this view, man has been saved from inner flatness, emptiness, and feelings of alienation through the vision of another world, a supernatural world, presided over by God. This present earthly world takes on its meaning through a kind of reflected glory. It was created by God. It was God's gift to man—or at least it is a world to be held in trust. Experience in this world is seen as a prelude to or preparation for *real living* in the supernatural world.

This image of God and the world has found expression in great art and literature. It is reflected in scripture and in many of the rituals of the church. The most familiar languages of faith grew out of this background. And so long as this image rings true for man, the attendant languages are quite acceptable. But it does not ring true for many men today.

Perhaps the single most important theological fact to be reckoned with in our time is the waning sense of the supernatural in the experience of modern man.

To many modern persons the varied languages of faith, instead of reflecting contemporary views of reality as being dynamic, of one order, relational, and evolutionary, seem to imply categories of the static and the self-contained. Modern man hears the languages of moral injunctions—fixed, firm, and absolute. But then he realizes that his own ethical decisions must often be made in highly fluid circumstances, where he can find no ideal solution and in which neat rules of procedure do not give the needed guidance. The shift from supernaturalism to a one-order perception of reality raises fundamental questions about matters of faith and morals and supremely about God. The shift from static to dynamic-relational categories requires not only a rethinking of the basic doctrines, but also languages which function effectively. With the ancient Hebrews the question might be asked, "How shall we sing the Lord's song in this new and strange land?"

In an awareness of the new situation in which we find ourselves, we shall explore some possibilities in affirming the reality of God. We shall look further into the languages of faith. We shall ask what it means to be a person of faith and hope in the twentieth century.

9.
The Christian Vision of God

GEORGE SANTAYANA made the interesting observation that "the attempt to speak without speaking any particular language is not more hopeless than the attempt to have a religion that shall be no religion in particular."[1] No one is ever religious "in general." Religion is a living and acting out of specific visions and understandings and commitments.

So it is when we speak of God within the context of religious faith. Speech about God is speech within the framework of some tradition or definable orientation. We do not talk about God in the abstract when we are using the word "God" in its religious sense.

In this chapter we shall move toward an interpretation of specifically Christian ways of speaking of God. Our ultimate purpose is to ask whether there are resources in the Christian tradition for modern man as he seeks a faith by which to live in the twentieth century. There are those who believe we have moved into a post-Christian era. Some regret this fact and others welcome it. Before passing judgment on that issue, it is well for us to recall the nature of the Christian vision and the

Christian languages. Only then will we be in a position to raise the question of contemporary relevance.

Jesus' Vision of God and Man

Consideration of the Christian vision of God begins with Jesus. Our records concerning Jesus are limited. Much of what we have is interpretation of events as remembered. Nevertheless, there are some things we can say with reasonable certainty about the life, teachings, and death of Jesus, and the major interpretations which were placed upon them in the early church.

It is not possible for us to participate in Jesus' inner life—his thoughts, feelings, purposes, aspirations as he personally experienced them. However, we can draw some inferences from what we know of his life, teachings, and relationships. To those who knew him best he was a sensitive, caring person with a profound sense of God's presence, providence, and purpose. He showed forth a feeling for the sanctity of existence, the dignity of human life, and the sovereignty of God. One sees in him the spirit of life-affirmation, belief in the human enterprise, conviction that life is of God.

There probably were no strictly new ideas in the teachings of Jesus. It was the way he expressed what he had to say, and the way his message was communicated in his attitude and his life, that brought the quality of novelty and freshness to his ministry. Courage, gentleness, and hope were combined in the living witness of his life. He not only imparted his vision of God and of the human situation, he himself became the vision for his devoted followers.

Jesus expressed the conviction that the world and all beings within the world are to be understood in relation to God. He was thoroughly Jewish in the conviction that "The earth is the Lord's and the fulness thereof, the world and those who dwell therein . . ." (PSALMS 24:1). He proclaimed that God is a God of love, justice, goodness, wisdom, and mercy. Affirming that God is vitally involved in human affairs, Jesus called men to repentance and righteousness in response to the will and requirements of God. Jesus accepted the Jewish belief that the will of God is made known in the Law, but he was no strict legalist in biblical interpretation and interpretation of the Law. He expressed profound concern for the needs of human beings, seeking to minister to them where they were. Jesus expressed a free spirit toward the scriptures in the light of his understanding of God's concern for men.

Jesus responded to persons as creatures of God, precious in his sight. He identified with outcasts and announced that he was sent to the lost sheep of the house of Israel. It is reported that the common people heard him gladly. His gospel was a gospel of redemption in witness to the God whose grace and goodness cannot be measured by human deserving. The parables of the lost coin, the lost sheep, and the lost son express the redemptive dimension of Jesus' message.

Jesus expressed a vision of hope through his life. The burden of his message was the coming of God's kingdom. This kingdom, expressing God's rule and sovereignty, is both present and future; it is already "in your midst," and still to come in its fullness. Man's whole life, he taught, is to be understood and lived in reference to the kingdom. Participation in the kingdom is the greatest good. The kingdom manifests God's rule over the universe.

In the light of the kingdom, Jesus called men to repentance and to ethical and religious righteousness. He stressed the importance of sincerity of purpose, humility of spirit, love of God and neighbor. Of such is the kingdom of God. Jesus finally gave his own life in total witness to his acceptance of God's claim on him, and in witness to the message of the kingdom. He spoke in the languages of word and deed.

A Vision of Wholeness

As one seeks to expose himself to the life and spirit and message of Jesus, one feels in it the quality of wholeness and wholesomeness. There is a vision and an outlook that cuts through ancient terminology and across cultural differences.

Jesus saw persons as persons. He permitted them to be persons. He saw them in relationship to each other, to the good earth, and to God. He saw all persons, including the outcast, in terms of their possibilities.

Jesus did not depreciate the natural and the physical. He spoke of creation as being of God. In teaching he frequently referred to common and natural things: the soil, the heavens, the sower, the mustard seed, workers in the vineyard, women making bread, harvest, rain, and sun. He found renewal in the out-of-doors. Jesus did not see body and spirit as being in basic conflict, one evil the other good. He saw man in wholeness.

He confronted the tragic fact of sin in human life. Yet, he placed a high estimate on man's moral powers. Apparently he regarded virtue as an achievement and not a supernatural gift imposed from above, and he assumed that persons have the capacity to make decisions, choosing the way of repentance and righteousness. In his own way Jesus affirmed that no man is an island unto himself. Men belong together in one human family as brothers, with God as Father. In mutual service man serves God and fellowman.

The vision of wholeness is manifest in Jesus' interpretation of the Kingdom of God. The kingdom is not a foreign reality to be imposed on man and the earth in some dramatic, apocalyptic fashion. To be sure, Jesus may have combined the apocalyptic hope with the Kingdom of God concept. This is debatable. But clearly there is a strain of the immanent in his teaching about the kingdom. It is already present; it is to grow and spread; it is not to come with visible signs.

Jesus spoke of God, the world, and man in their interrelatedness. Reconciliation with God and reconciliation with man were parts of one pattern. Life is fulfilled in love of God and neighbor. Love of God is manifest in the whole person—with heart, soul, strength, and mind. Love of neighbor is not simply love of one's own kind, as the parable of the Good Samaritan makes clear. His ethical teachings are rooted in God's love, goodness, and mercy together with love of neighbor. Running through all these teachings is the vision of a basic unity in God. Human relationships are seen in a pattern of wholeness, mutual concern, and service. The God-man relationship is perceived as bearing on one's whole life in a world created by God.

To appreciate the depth and wonder of Jesus' vision of life we need only to compare it with some alternative perspectives: world-denying and world-resenting; cynical perspectives issuing in life styles of exploitation or cruel indifference; perspectives providing for no abiding trust or hope, leaving man a restless, anxious creature seizing upon such fleeting satisfactions as he can find. In communicating his vision Jesus gave people another world to live in, putting all things in a different light.

The Vision and Hope of the Early Church

The message of the early Christian church was not simply a continuation of Jesus' proclamation of the Kingdom of God. The impact of Jesus' career was such that his faithful followers came to associate him with God's presence and saving work. Since they were accustomed to thinking of God's supreme saving work in Messianic terms, it is not surprising that they adopted Messiah language in relationship to Jesus, affirming, "He is the Messiah (the Christ)."

In the early church the message of the Kingdom of God

was reinterpreted in the light of Jesus' role as revealer and redeemer. In Jesus' life, death, and resurrection, together with the gift of the Holy Spirit, God was bringing in the new age. The long-awaited salvation was in course. In the light of its immanent consummation men were called to repentance, righteousness, and faith. The God of creation was now supremely revealed in Jesus Christ: ". . . the God who said 'Let light shine out of darkness,' . . . has shone in our hearts to give the light of the knowledge of the glory of God in the face of Christ" (II Corinthians 4:6).

In the light of Jesus' death it was necessary to reinterpret the Messianic image in reference to him. It had not been anticipated that the Messiah would die, certainly not on a cross. The early church found an explanation of the mystery of Jesus' death in the unpreparedness of the people of Israel and their rejection of him. Thus, the kingdom must wait, and the early church found its mission in calling men to repentance and recognition of Jesus' messiahship. In the fullness of time, the Messiah would return in glory. The early church was a witnessing, waiting, hoping community.

The Continuing Christian Vision

Years passed, but Jesus did not return as had been expected. Theological reinterpretations again were called for. As it became evident that the new age might not come soon, the early church gave greater attention to formulating statements of faith and to creating an organization to care for continuing needs.

For nineteen centuries there have been those who have continued to define the ultimate Christian hope in terms of Christ's immanent return in glory and the sudden establishment of his kingdom. Others have reinterpreted the Christian hope. At times the promise of a blessed immortality has been central in the Christian statement of hope. Other formulations of the hope have stressed the promise of forgiveness of sins, moral transformation, participation in a new being, and the Christianization of the social order.

Although there have been many expressions of the Christian hope, there has been a persistent claim that the God made known in Jesus Christ is to be trusted in life and death; in him is a living hope. The final word about God and the world is not one of condemnation and despair but a word of grace and hope. Man's ultimate hope is grounded in God: Creator, Redeemer, Life-giving Spirit.

The Christian message claims to be the deepest wisdom about life flowing from the most authentic vision of God. It comes as a perspective on life in its farthest reaches. It claims to speak to the ultimate issues, setting the whole range of human experiences in an order of meaning and hope. Even though Christians have differed among themselves on many points—including the most appropriate formulation of the Christian hope—there has been a persistent appeal to God made known supremely in Jesus Christ. This is the distinctive witness of the Christian faith. The continuing Christian vision is the vision of God whose creative power is declared in nature, whose redeeming love is made known in Christ, whose comforting, instructing, guiding presence is manifest through his indwelling spirit. In the light of that vision the Christian comes to a new understanding of himself and of the meaning of his life.

Through the centuries many attempts have been made to set forth the vision in formal statements of faith and systems of theology. One of the classic theological doctrines directed to this end is the doctrine of the Trinity. But the languages of Christian faith most widely heard, grasped, and responded to are of a different kind. They are indirect languages, in which the presence and work of God is declared in connection with a person, a drama, and a community of faith. Because so much of the gripping power of Christianity is related to this language —and because some of the greatest challenges to Christian faith are now directed at the meaningfulness of this language —we need to consider it with care.

10.

Christian Imagery: Resource and Stumbling Block

THE CHRISTIAN vision and message have come to multitudes of persons with transforming power. Indeed, the course of history has been changed through that vision and message.

We have spoken of the importance of the language of religion. The Christian impact cannot be understood without reference to the specific languages which have been used. Imagery of tremendous expressive and evoking power has communicated the Christian vision of hope, a hope grounded in the living God who acts in history.

In affirming the reality of God, Christian faith has kept pointing in three related directions: (1) to the revealing person; (2) to the revealing-interpreting drama of salvation; (3) to the witnessing-serving-reconciling community which is the church. In affirming the reality of God and the wonder of hope, Christian faith has spoken of the person, the drama, and the community of faith. For centuries Christians have testified that they have come to a new life of faith and hope in relationship with the person, the drama, and the community of faith. God, they have affirmed, has been experienced in these ways.

In reference to each, doctrines have been formulated, insights into God's dealings with men have been expressed, rich imagery has been employed, a way of seeing the human situation has been communicated, a way of life has been encouraged.

In presenting its vision and message, Christianity has spoken in deeply personal terms. All history is interpreted in relation to the will and purposes of the Divine Person. The supreme revelation of God is declared to be found in the person of Jesus Christ. In discussing the role of models in theological discourse, and the Christian appeal to the personal model, Frederick Ferré has written:

> Theological speech projects a model of immense responsive significance, drawn from "the facts" as the key to its conceptual significance. This model, for theism, is made up of the "spiritual" characteristics of personality: will, purpose, wisdom, love, and the like. For Christianity, more specifically, the conceptual model consists in the creative, self-giving, personal love of Jesus Christ. In this model is found the only literal meaning which these terms, like "creative," "personal," and "love," can have in the Christian vocabulary. All the concepts of the Christian are organized and synthesized in relation to this model. The efforts of systematic theology are bent to explicating the consistency and coherence of the synthesis built on this model of "God" as key concept. Christian preaching is devoted to pointing out the applicability of this conceptual synthesis to common experiences of life.[1]

To understand the distinctive Christian language, we must understand this characteristic personal model as it is brought to bear upon the revealing person, the revealing-interpreting drama, and the witnessing-serving-saving community of faith. The distinctive Christian affirmations of God and hope are wrapped up in this language and manner of communicating.

We have called attention to the expressive and evoking power of Christian imagery. We must now go on to say that it is this imagery and the interpretations placed on it which is creating serious problems for many persons today. The originating vision of God and wholeness and hope is lost, for many, in an imagery which fails to communicate with persons in a scientific age. Fundamentally, it is again the problem of supernaturalism. The traditional Christian imagery and attendant interpretations presuppose the language of supernaturalism, and it is this supernaturalism that confuses growing numbers of persons. Let us see how the language of Christian faith has pointed to profound insights, but now confronts major difficulty in "coming through" to the contemporary mind.

The Revealing Person

At the heart of Christianity's message is a person. The creator-God of Old Testament faith is presupposed, but, according to Christian faith, it is in the revealing person of Jesus Christ that the redeeming love of God is manifest.

Every faith confronts the problem of mediation. How does God draw near to man? How and where is God experienced in the concrete? In Christianity, appeal is made to mediating agents in nature ("the heavens declare the glory of God") but supremely to Jesus as the Christ.

The power of Christianity is in large measure the evoking power of the figure of Jesus, exemplifying love of God and neighbor. He not only proclaimed the vision of wholeness and of hope; for multitudes he has become the vision. Paul expressed the faith of millions when he said, "God was in Christ reconciling the world to himself . . ." (II CORINTHIANS 5:19). In Christ the vision of the reconciling, uniting, healing, whole-making God has broken in upon men with compelling power.

In our own time Alfred North Whitehead has written movingly of the evoking power of Jesus as the revealing person. Recalling that Plato came to the conviction that the divine element in the world is to be conceived as a persuasive rather than a coercive agency, Whitehead wrote:

> This doctrine should be looked upon as one of the greatest intellectual discoveries in the history of religions. . . . The essence of Christianity is the appeal to the life of Christ as a revelation of the nature of God and of his agency in the world. . . . there can be no doubt as to what elements in the record have evoked a response from all that is best in human nature. The Mother, the Child, and the bare manger: the lowly man, homeless and self-forgetful, with his message of peace, love, and sympathy: the suffering, the agony, the tender words as life ebbed, the final despair: and the whole with the authority of supreme victory.
>
> I need not elaborate. Can there be any doubt that the power of Christianity lies in its revelation in act, of that which Plato divined in theory?[2]

Jesus became to his followers such a unique source of spiritual insight and transforming power that they found revealed in him that which is most divine in the universe as a whole. His faithful followers have said in effect, "He brings God to us. In him we experience the presence of the God who gives new life." For them Jesus in his own being declared the reality of the God of wholeness and of hope.

Unfortunately, through the centuries theologians and interpreters have often obscured the Jesus of history with his vision of wholeness and of hope. They have dressed him in metaphysical garb, debated as to whether the Son was of the *same* substance as that of the Father; they have interpreted him as a preexistent, supernatural agent of individual and cosmic redemption; they have formulated Christologies which would have completely baffled Jesus. It was essential that Christologies, interpreting the person and work of Christ, should be formulated. It was not essential that in the process the picture of Jesus as remembered in the early church should have been lost as it often was.

We can understand what happened. Endeavoring to use contemporary philosophical ideas in the interpretation of Jesus, theologians sometimes adopted dualistic ways of thinking. Body and spirit, God and world were seen as belonging to very different orders. In the stress upon basic cleavages in man and universe, the vision of interrelatedness and wholeness tended to be lost. Amos Wilder puts it this way:

> This tendency toward otherworldliness in Christianity has, of course, a long history. In ancient Israel there was no cleavage between body and soul, nor between man and nature. The soul could not be redeemed without the body, and man could not be redeemed by taking him out of nature. But the Greek world had become increasingly conscious of the gulf between nature and spirit. The tension between the two led in the Hellenistic period to a craving for release *from* nature and *from* the flesh, by all manner of religious disciplines, by meditation, asceticism, and sacrament. This outlook impressed itself upon early Christianity in various forms, good and bad, and tended to obscure the biblical wholeness and realism.[3]

It is one of the anomalies of Christian history that in the attempt to clarify and give systematic statement to the meaning of Jesus Christ for man, the wonder of his own transforming vision should often have been obscured. Although lip service has been given to his humanity, its real meaning has been compromised by an other-worldly interpretation of his divinity.

Acceptance of doctrines about him came to be more important than sharing with the revealing person in his vision of God and wholeness and hope.

Is it not significant in our own time, when increasing numbers of persons report that the traditional supernaturalistic Christologies mean little or nothing to them, that people keep turning to the picture of Jesus himself as one who communicated a vision of God and life and wholeness? His life, as remembered in the early church, has a way of speaking now.

But there are difficulties here also. We are separated from Jesus in many ways. We live in a different culture and in a different age. It is not easy for persons living in a technological, scientific, urban culture to identify with one who lived in small communities of first-century Palestine. We desperately need his vision and his spirit, but we also need to find his spirit embodied in our midst again and again. In the language of Luther, we need persons who are as Christ to their neighbor. The Christ reality is not confined to one point in ancient history. It appears again and again wherever the reconciling, healing, life-giving reality which was in Jesus appears in our midst where life is struggling for integrity and meaning and hope.

The Revealing-Interpreting Drama

In affirming the reality of God, Christianity not only points to the revealing person, it points to a sublime drama—inviting man to see himself in relationship to movements and purposes of cosmic importance. There are fundamental themes running through the Christian drama: creation, providence, judgment, sin, redemption (through divine incarnation, death, resurrection), new life in a new community marked by faith, hope, and love and life in mission. In this drama man is invited to see the meaning of existence in its wholeness. However mysterious

God may be, Christianity affirms that he is revealed in this drama as a God who acts in history creatively and redemptively, coming to man in judgment and in grace, calling man into a new life in a new community.

The Christian drama draws heavily on the heritage of Judaism. God is portrayed creating the world, manifesting his sovereignty over the universe. Man in self-will asserts his own sovereignty in opposition to God's. In righteous judgment God brings punishment to those who resist his claims, but offers promise to those who are willing to enter into covenant with him, to be a chosen-serving people of God. According to the Christian drama, God's promises are fulfilled in the coming of Christ, in whom redemption is effected, and man is offered a new life in a new community.

It is a drama centering in mighty acts of God, many of them associated with crises in the lives of individuals and peoples. It is a revealing drama, in the sense that men of faith discern God's presence, power, and purposes manifest in specific events of judgment, deliverance, and summons such as the exodus from Egypt and the resurrection of Jesus. It is a drama presenting a picture of the whole story, a theology of history.

For centuries many of the greatest artists, poets, musicians have drawn their themes from the Christian drama of creation, estrangement, and redemption. Systems of theology have been written seeking to set forth its meaning in doctrinal form. Sermons have been preached and books written calling men to live in the light of the vision of this drama. Birth and death and all that lies between are seen in a dimension of wonder and profundity and eternal purpose in the perspective of this dramatic vision. Historically, there can be no question about the transforming power of this drama.

But a perceptible change is taking place in the modern world. Fewer persons recognize themselves within the drama as set forth. It is as though something terribly important is there, but one is not gripped by it. Great art may attend it, but one is not shaken in the depths of his being, inspired with a new vision, or called to commitment. If the drama speaks, it speaks of a vision that has vanished.

So here again one feels that something precious is getting away from modern man. It is not that he has become literal-minded and cannot hear messages that come in myth and metaphor and varied symbols. It is the strange feeling that the drama is talking about something that is not actually real. And many modern men wish to face the facts.

Since Christianity has done so much of its talking about God through the imagery of this drama, those who are not finding themselves within it are wondering if there is anything to the Christian idea of God—or to any idea of God at all, for that matter. The drama was intended to communicate a vision of God and of hope and of wholeness, but in the midst of all the supernatural trappings that attend the drama, the vision fades. Many persons ask: Could it be that God is just an imaginary element in an outgrowth myth?

We stand at a point of crisis. Man needs a vision of greatness by which to live. Some imaginative, dramatic expression of the vision is required for today, lest the transforming light be reduced to a set of rules or propositions. The classic Christian drama has provided such a vehicle of expression. But with radically changed views of man and the universe, the Christian picture is being called into question.

The Witnessing-Serving-Reconciling Community of Faith

To be a Christian, we are told, is not simply an individual matter. It is to be in the community or fellowship of the faithful; indeed, it is *to be* the body of Christ. Christian speaking of God involves speaking of God's spiritual presence, power, and work in the company of those who are seeking, finding, and sharing a new life in Christ.

To be in the Christian community is to participate in a history, to share in the insights, interpretations, values, and aspirations attendant upon that history. It is to find personal meaning through identification with decisive events and personalities in that history. It is to share in the languages of the community, including languages of theological interpretation and ritual. It is to be with like-minded followers of Jesus Christ in witness and in service. It is to be entrusted with the ministry of reconciliation which brings healing and wholeness and hope to men.

In a world in which there is so much of loneliness, depersonalization, association without depth, lack of communication, the very idea of such a witnessing-serving-reconciling community is wondrous. Can it exist in fact?

If the transforming reality experienced in the Christian movement is mediated through the revealing person and the revealing drama, it has also been mediated through the fellowship of those who have been gathered together in a common devotion to Jesus Christ. Here the grace of God has been and is experienced by many persons.

A part of the task of theology is to provide a theological interpretation of the church. This work has been going on from the time of Paul. Varied theories have been developed indicating how the church is implicated in the mediation and communication of God's grace. These interpretations reveal that there are varied perceptions of the church and its ministry. Current ecumenical discussion revolves around these varied perceptions with the attendant variations in language.

Who can doubt that a very considerable part of the power of Christianity lies in its vision and experience of the witnessing-serving-reconciling community? But who can doubt that some of the most searching questions about the contemporary reality and relevance of Christianity come to focus at the point of the church?

Here again the specter of a prescientific kind of otherworldliness comes into view. Many of the more familiar doctrines of the church presuppose views of man and the universe which do not communicate meaningfully with modern man. The situation is complicated by attitudes and values often manifest in organized religion. The contrast is great between the vision of the witnessing-serving-reconciling community and what one often finds in the actual church.

Christian talk about God involves the presence and work of God in the church. Such talk does not always come through loudly and clearly. What the church says about God in her formal teachings is often confusing. What the church says about God in her rituals often implies an outdated otherworldliness. What the church says about God through her life in the world does not always add up to a vision of greatness and wholeness and reconciliation. The honest seeker has been led to think that it is the *church* which is best qualified to speak of the reality of God. But increasing numbers of thoughtful persons wonder if this is the way it really is.

One form which the question is now taking has to do with the relationship of the witnessing-serving-reconciling fellowship to the church as an institution. Are we to believe that they are synonymous? Or is there today a basic conflict between the two, so that we must look for the true community of faith outside organized religion? Or do we find authentic fellowships of faith within the organized church, but only fragmentarily and fleetingly? Or are we to think of the function of the organized church as that of creating conditions and structures which hopefully will issue in the witnessing-serving-reconciling community?

In raising these questions we are not only talking about an

institution. We are talking about how God is real and present and active in our corporate life. We seek a vision of greatness and of wholeness. There is reason to believe that whatever meaning God may have for modern man, it has to do with such a vision. But does the church lead men to this vision in this time?

Toward Creative, Contemporary Theology

The situation in Christendom seems to be something like this: Through a series of events, centering in Jesus and the community of faith which came into being around him, a vision of transforming power broke forth in human history. It was a wondrous vision of hope having to do with God and man and human possibilities.

As Christians from the earliest times have endeavored to express their new and deepened understandings of God and man and human destiny, they have turned to the languages of doctrine and of drama. In formulating the doctrines and in giving expression to the drama, they have inevitably used thought-forms of their day.

On a deeply personal level, Christians have spoken of how they have come to a new relationship with God and into a new life of faith and hope and love through the revealing person of Jesus Christ and through the witnessing-serving-reconciling community of faith (the church). Again, they have used thought-forms of their times and places in setting forth their understandings of the deeper meanings of the revealing person and the community of faith.

We have now come into a period of history in which many of the thought-forms used in past theological work seem obsolete. The transforming vision and the experiences of disclosure and commitment associated with the revealing person and the community of faith are often lost or obscured in the interpretations which are placed upon them. Because modern man so frequently regards time-honored Christian languages and interpretations as being outmoded, he becomes skeptical about the whole Christian message. It is not easy to extricate the vision and the experiences from the forms in which they are expressed. On the contrary, they often seem to be inextricably interwoven.

The problem has come to focus on the doctrine of God. Christians have always witnessed to their faith that the new life they have come to know in Jesus Christ and in the community of faith is truly *from God*. Through the centuries Christian theologians have therefore directed a major part of their attention to setting forth doctrines of God which would be faithful to the experience and testimony of the historic community of faith. As time has passed, the impression has grown that the heart of Christianity is to be found in its doctrines of God as formulated in historic creeds, confessions, and systems of thought.

It is here that much of the challenge to the truth of Christian doctrine is to be found at the present time. The widely held and long-held image of God as a supernatural being who once brought the world into being by divine fiat and who now orders it and the affairs of men from a dwelling place beyond the world is not taken seriously by many persons today. The drama of God's redemptive work through the substitutionary work of his Son, bringing those who respond to an eternal life of joy and fulfillment while those who do not respond are left to an eternal destiny of estrangement, no longer moves many men who see little relevance in such views for the problems of today's world.

The question emerges: Are the Christian vision and the Christian experience of a new life of faith, hope, and love really dependent upon the images of God so frequently associated with Christian thought in the past? Could it be that what is really crucial in Christian seeing and valuing and trusting and hoping and loving and aspiring can better be understood in other ways? Could it be that a more contemporary understanding of the reality of God might not only illuminate the experiences of Christians in the past, but also illuminate man's present situation as he seeks a way of hope in his world?

A great deal of contemporary theology turns on this question. There are those who would call us back to traditional modes of thought. There are those who would avoid direct talk about God, preferring to talk about human possibilities. There are those who would keep the traditional imagery and language, interpreting its contemporary meaning through demythologizing or remythologizing.

Still another approach is being taken by those who believe that if Christianity is to make its greatest possible contribution to the religious life of man in this new day, it must show how it is possible to affirm the reality of God in a way that is meaningful in the contemporary situation and that points toward a life of hope in the midst of the complexities of the modern world. There are contemporary Christian theologians who are profoundly concerned that the heart of the Christian vision and experience of new life should be re-presented to modern man as an authentic possibility. But, they are convinced, this requires a new conceptualization of God which reflects the deepest understandings and experiences of persons living today. There are those who believe that only in relation to such a new conceptualization of God can the deeper contemporary relevance of the revealing person, the interpreting drama, and the witnessing-serving-reconciling community of faith be grasped by many modern persons in their quest for the significant life in a technological age.

11.
Can New Ground Be Broken in Theology?

IT IS REPORTED that Einstein was once asked what led to some of his revolutionary theories. He replied, "I challenged an axiom." It is the thesis of this chapter that the time has come to examine and challenge many long held theological axioms. The knowledge and cultural revolutions of our times have created a new situation for mankind. Religion cannot and should not escape the searchlight of inquiry which is falling on every area of life.

The age-old questions pertaining to the meaning of life, the nature and destiny of man, the status of value in the universe, and the grounds of human hope continue to be asked. But they are asked in a new situation. Man brings many new understandings to his questioning. He sees his world and himself in new relationships. Thus, while the old questions continue to be asked, they are reformulated in the context of new perceptions of man and the universe, and in the midst of profound cultural changes.

In many fields it is being found necessary to devise new conceptual tools with which to work. In science, art, political and ethical theory, institutional life, and virtually every other aspect of life, men are seeking new concepts and images and organizing tools appropriate to the highly dynamic situations in which we live.

Can new ground be broken in theology? There is no easy answer to this question. There are those who insist that the basic issues and the possible approaches to them were spelled out long ago, that there can be nothing really new under the theological sun. They grant that challenging axioms is fine in most areas of life, but insist it is of the nature of religion and theological truth to be unchanging.

Other persons, however, would agree with Alfred North Whitehead when he wrote, "Religion will not regain its old power until it can face change in the same spirit as does science. Its principles may be eternal, but the expression of those principles requires continual development."[1] Unless religion and theology are to be relegated to some pigeonhole of irrelevancy, it is imperative that their axioms be examined, and where indicated, new approaches sought.

The time has passed when religion and theology can be studied in isolation from the rest of what is going on in the world. In his quest for the significant life, man turns to many fields of investigation for information and guidance. Unless he can see how religion and theology are related to the processes and problems of life-orientation, human relationships, and decision-making, he will not have much interest in them. More specifically, modern man is not very much interested in hearing how God can be efficacious in delivering him from the world. He *may* be interested in hearing how God is relevant in relating him to the world more creatively and meaningfully. It is essential that theology adopt more of an experimental, venturing-out stance. Having defined his problems, the theologian needs to engage in experimental work, trying out various lines of thought and investigation. His methods are different from those of the scientist, but the spirit of inquiry and the readiness to keep trying to find the more fruitful hypotheses are essential in both science and theology.

In the remainder of this chapter, three theological problem-areas will be named in which axioms need to be challenged and new approaches need to be found. These are not the only important problem-areas in contemporary theology, but attendant upon them are some of the most crucial issues confronting theology today. It is in connection with some of these problem-areas that significant breakthroughs in understanding are badly needed. The issues revolve around the relation of science and religion, the waning sense of the supernatural, the movement from static to dynamic-relational-evolutionary views of reality.

Clarifying the Relation of Science and Religion

A gradual change has taken place in modern man's perceptions of the relation of science and religion: from conflict to coexistence to communication.

The era in which the conflict between science and religion was discussed is pretty well past. Next came the period of peaceful coexistence. There were those who resolved the alleged conflict by assigning science and religion their respective roles, and letting it go at that. For example, it was said that science deals with *facts* whereas religion deals with *values*. Or it was said that science deals with perceptible and measurable phenomena whereas religion is concerned with the realm of the intangible and "spiritual." In various ways it was insisted that there is no basic conflict between science and religion. They can go their separate ways.

It is now quite clear that at best this solution was only a temporary help. Granted that science and religion have their respective problems, methods, and languages, they still function in the same world and deal with the same people.

The neat separation between science and religion has come at a high price. Scientific knowledge and religious values have come to be sharply separated in the lives of many human beings; indeed, there is a split in our culture. We have not learned how to relate scientific knowledge and skills with the disciplines, values, and hopes born of the religious vision. Thus, we have knowledge without wisdom, power without enlightened purpose.

For centuries man has lived with the notion that certain sharp divisions permeate the world of our experience: between body and mind, sacred and secular, natural and supernatural, material and spiritual, and so on. Perceiving reality in this divided way, man has found it impossible to achieve a view of life and the world in its wholeness and organic character. Life is seen under the image of division.

In the midst of the conflicts, frustrations, and alienations which complicate the human situation, man needs a vision of wholeness enabling him to see his life and destiny in relationship to the vast cosmic drama. Such a vision might help him achieve greater inner harmony, a new sense of the relatedness of all human beings, and a fuller awareness of the whole of which all particular things are parts and from which he cannot resign. Such a vision hopefully would reflect not only the awesome knowledge of science but the values and hopes which attend religious insight and experience.

If man is to move toward such a vision of wholeness, there must be a drawing together of insights from various fields. Even though science and religion have their specialized tasks to perform and their distinctive contributions to make, there must be increasing communication between the scientific and the religious communities.

Insofar as the word "God" suggests or points toward a reality of wholeness, relating all beings, the theologian ought to be deeply concerned about communication among all persons studying the world in which man lives. Unfortunately, some theologians assume that theology is an autonomous field of study and can go it alone. This assumption needs to be challenged.

It is in the decision-making situations of life, where basic values are at stake, that we now experience the tragedy of separating too neatly the knowledge and power born of science and the vision and commitment born of mature religion. C. A. Coulson, British mathematician, has written:

> These problems—the control of nuclear explosion, the control of world population, the feeding of hungry men and women, the use and abuse of methods of mass communication—are all problems where a theological critique needs to be made; and it must be made within the context of biology, sociology, and physics.[2]

Theology is now called upon to show how the analytical, descriptive, and predictive work of science is relevant to the unitive, evaluative, and redemptive functions of religion.[3] The possibility of new ground being broken in theology depends upon the readiness of theologians and other religious leaders to think in these terms so that the vision of God may illuminate life in its wholeness, bringing a vision of hope.

Coming to Terms With the Passing of Traditional Supernaturalism

Nature has come to a new status in our time. The idea of a supernatural realm over and above the natural order, with another set of causes, is seriously questioned, and by many persons rejected. Belief in miracle, in the sense of intervention in the processes of this world by a supernatural agency, is fading. Explanations are sought within man, society, and nature. Astronomer Harlow Shapley, for example, writes of "the growing conviction that appeal to the supernatural is unnecessary for the beginning and evolution of living organisms."[4]

What we are witnessing is not simply the waning sense of the supernatural. Of equal or greater importance is the emergence of revised concepts of nature. Increasingly, nature is believed to be dynamic, interrelated, evolutionary, and open-ended. In this view nature is not limited to physical and biological structures; it includes human history. Ideas, ideals, aspirations, love, creative art, and the spiritual dimensions of man are regarded, not as being foreign to the natural order, but as representing its flowering out.

The newer views tend toward a one-order theory of reality. This one order is regarded as being highly complex (possibly involving levels) but with an interrelationship of parts. There is both continuity and creativity in the order of nature, according to this view.

The waning sense of the supernatural is apparent in secularization which Harvey Cox has defined as "man turning his attention from the worlds beyond and toward this world and this time."[5] Increasingly we live in a secular culture in which the supernatural and symbols of the supernatural mean less and less. The distinction between the sacred and the secular is difficult to maintain under these circumstances.

There are persons of religious interest who bemoan secularization and the waning sense of the supernatural. There are others who welcome these developments in the conviction that they open the way to a new and creative chapter in human history. From this point of view, it is time for man to move beyond the immaturities and dependencies which belief in supernaturalism often encouraged. Man is now called upon to play a role of increasing responsibility as he takes his place in the universe.

But even among those who welcome the coming of secularization there are some who are convinced that danger attends man in his new situation. It is the danger of losing the awareness of the dimension of the transcendent. Supernaturalism enlarged the individual's frame of orientation. It provided a framework of meaning which transcended the perceptible and measurable. It suggested values and destinies not realized in the immediate situation. It gave man a larger world to live in and opened the door to a hope not immediately fulfilled. There are those who welcome the passing of supernaturalism in its traditional, cosmological sense. At the same time there are those who believe we need a functional equivalent for supernaturalism, disclosing a transcendent dimension to existence in the secular world. George Santayana was correct in his assertion that religion opens vistas which provide "another world to live in." But that other world need not be discontinuous from the world of present experience. On the contrary, it may include present experience, seen and understood in the light of a more comprehensive frame of orientation and devotion.

It is in pointing the way to a new vision of transcendence—a functional equivalent for supernaturalism—that contemporary theology now meets one of its greatest challenges. It is time to question the long-held axiom that theology deals exclusively with the supernatural. It is also time for theology to show how the vision of God is both possible and relevant in the experience of secular man.

Moving Toward Dynamic-Relational-Evolutionary Concepts of Reality

Bishop John A. T. Robinson has written, ". . . we need not fear flux: God is in the rapids as much as in the rocks, and as Christians we are free to swim and not merely to cling."[6] In these words Bishop Robinson has pointed toward a new way of thinking in our time and toward a religious problem which attends that new way of thinking.

Briefly stated, modern man experiences and interprets life in dynamic-relational-evolutionary ways and images. Modern man is on the move in a world of eventfulness. Traditional religion, however, has pictured the world in more static terms. Things are what they are within themselves. Relations are regarded as being incidental. The life of faith is interpreted as a life of security and certainty. The question modern man now faces is: How does one find a religious interpretation of life together with religious resources and guidelines in a world of flux, of complex relationships, of never-ending becoming? Obviously, there is new ground to be broken in reference to these matters.

In traditional theology God was thought of as a perfect, self-sufficient, unchanging being. Man was thought of as a creature of fixed properties, consisting of soul *and* body. Salvation was regarded as being absolute (rather than relative), involving forgiveness of sins, transformation of an evil nature into a new nature or disposition, the winning of a blessed immortality. The God-world relationship was interpreted in over-under images. God touched the world through imposition or intervention.

As early Christian theologians spelled out these ideas in doctrinal form, they frequently used the philosophical concept of "substance" as a working tool. The concept of substance implies that the reality of anything involves an underlying, unchanging substance in which qualities inhere. Thus, one might speak of a divine substance and a human substance. The Nicene theologians, defining divinity in terms of substance, discussed the divinity of Christ by asking if the Son were of the same substance as the Father. Thus the philosophical-theology of the early centuries of the Christian movement tended to translate what was living and dynamic in human experience into static categories of thought and doctrine. Modern man has inherited doctrinal systems presupposing these static categories.

In the present era man increasingly thinks of reality in dynamic terms. The sciences perceive matter and life, not in terms of substance, but in terms of process. Dynamic and relational views of personality are taken for granted. Man is seen as a creature in relationship. No being exists in isolation. Things come into being in a dynamic matrix of events and relations.

The time has come to challenge the axiom that theology deals only with the fixed, the permanent, the unchanging. The time has come to seek an understanding of the meaning of God in relation to a dynamic, relational, and evolutionary world, and to re-think the doctrines of God, man, salvation (and related doctrines) in terms which reflect contemporary perceptions of the way things are.

It has long been assumed that security and significance are found in relationship to the fixed and unchanging. Much of our religious symbolism embodies this assumption. We now need creative theological work showing how there are resources for a sense of at-homeness and significance *in the midst of* the dynamic, relational, and becoming dimensions of reality. Instead of seeking the security of fixed and final points or events, we need to seek patterns of integrity which combine flux with dependability. In the search for a meaningful, contemporary conception of God, theologians need to seek structures and processes of dependability and directionality in which persons can trust and to which they can relate. The God symbol ought to kindle an awareness of and illuminate in contemporary terms the way things ultimately are and the way things work out.

Earlier it was suggested that the God-idea is the idea of an ultimate, objective ground of faith and hope. It was also suggested that the crucial God-question is: In what sense, if any, can we meaningfully affirm that there is that in reality which corresponds to the God-idea? Modern man now asks that God-question in a world which he experiences and interprets in dynamic-relational-evolutionary ways. That which he experiences as being most real and determinative in his experience —that which he keeps coming to and up against in his living— is implicated in the complex processes in which human life is set.

Historically the vision of God has brought a vision of hope. Traditional religion has thought of a perfect, self-sufficient, unchanging God, essentially apart from the world. The hope was that of deliverance from the limitations of the flesh and world. If one is prepared to recognize the passing of traditional supernaturalism, and if one is prepared to acknowledge the essentially dynamic, relational, evolutionary character of reality as experienced, then a fundamental rethinking of the God reality and the nature of religious hope is called for.

The problems in theological rethinking and reconstruction are many and complex. This is a time to keep working at the task, trying out various lines of thought experimentally, sharing perspectives. This is not a time in which to expect clear and final answers to complex theological questions. It is a time for recognizing the need for breaking new ground in theology.

12.
Affirming the Reality of God: Four Contemporary Approaches

IN THIS CHAPTER we shall consider the thought of several theologians who are keenly aware of contemporary currents of thought. They are concerned with the God-question. They are convinced that modern theology must endeavor to speak to the modern mind. They are convinced that theology must take into account newer perceptions of man and the universe in affirming the reality of God. However, they take different approaches in formulating the God-question and in affirming the reality of God.

The list of positions and theologians to be presented is not exhaustive. Some highly significant contemporary theologians will not even be mentioned. Those who are mentioned will be dealt with briefly. The purpose of this chapter is simply to suggest some of the various ways in which the reality of God is being affirmed in our time. All the theologians to be considered are identified with the Christian tradition and in varying degrees employ Christian imagery. Significant theological work is being done by other theologians as well. However, the scope of our study must be limited in some way. Furthermore, there is something to be said for the attempt to find growing edges within a specific tradition. The theologians to be considered presuppose a Judeo-Christian heritage, yet all are open to insights coming from any source promising new light on the question of God.

God as Supernatural Personal Spirit

In the midst of what they recognize as the waning sense of supernaturalism, there are those theologians who would reaffirm the reality of the supernatural God. There is no reason, they insist, why theology should give ground on the traditional view that God is other than and more than the space-time natural order. They affirm that it is not only possible but desirable to link the newer views of nature with belief in the supernatural God.

Nels F. S. Ferré is representative of this point of view. He is appreciative of the process philosophy of Alfred North Whitehead. He insists, however, that such philosophical understanding has its fullest relevance for theology only within ". . . a Christ-centered, evangelical supernaturalism based on revelation, which can be found only by faith. . . ."[1] He seeks to show how process philosophy is compatible with the structure of classical Christian faith.

Ferré searches for a formulation of a Christian doctrine of God which will provide a basis for a coherent interpretation of all experience and which is religiously meaningful. He speaks of God as the ground and goal of faith, the ultimate nature and purpose of existence.

He comes at his affirmation of God by way of the Christian revelation of God as *agape*, creating, self-disclosing, self-giving, unqualified love. Love, says Ferré, is the category of categories, including being, becoming, personality, spirit. He defines love as "the form of being which acts out of complete concern not only for all, in all dimensions of life, and the conditions which sustain, promote and enhance life, but also for ever new life and new conditions of life."[2]

God's perfect love leads him to create. God needs a world for his creative and redemptive activity. It is Ferré's judgment that Alfred North Whitehead has provided a highly perceptive description and analysis of the natural order as process and as organism. However, Ferré insists, nature is to be understood in reference to God; God is not explained in terms of nature: ". . . nature . . . is always the complement of creative love and of nonbeing. Nature is God's external agent through which he communicates with us directly and indirectly."[3] Thus, Ferré combines the idea of a supernatural God, known as personal Spirit, with a view of nature understood in processive terms.

According to Ferré, it is in classical Christianity that we find the structures of thought which most adequately encompass the truth of God and God's relation to the world. He agrees that knowledge has much light to throw on the world-order in which we live, and that in the light of this knowledge some long-held ideas may have to be discarded. But, he says, this does not invalidate the essential truth of the classical Christian position which he describes as follows:

> Classical Christianity affirms a living God who ultimately is creator, controller, and completer of human history as well as of the conditions necessary for it. Its God is supernatural. He sent his only Son in the fulness of time to die for the world's sin and to give eternal life by his conquest of death through the resurrection of his Son from the dead. Man is a fallen creature who can find salvation and eternal life, now and after death, only by believing in Christ and appropriating his work on man's behalf. Faith in such a God rests either in the authority of the Church, a supernatural institution, or in the authority of the Bible, the deposit of a supernatural revelation.[4]

It would appear that belief in God as Ferré conceives him would be compatible with any set of circumstances in the created world. Presumably God could use them all in relation to his loving purposes. Ferré writes:

> The idiot child, for that matter, is no problem to those who know life to be immortal so that the idiot child has as much time left for learning as does any one of us. God is never limited by time. He has all there is and can come to be! The reason that such an idiot is born into this world *may* be due to a number of chance circumstances in nature with no immediate moral relevance or direct purpose. That child, however, *may* be born for the sake of the family; for the sake of society; for some sake which we cannot now see.[5]

Thus God is absolutely sovereign, transcending all limitation. The person of faith knows that in the end God saves all things. God wins a "total victory." Thus, hope is held out, not only for a meaningful life in the present, but for a life of fulfillment after death.

It would be difficult to imagine a more hopeful philosophy or theology than that which Ferré presents. Not only does Christian faith provide hope, it also is said to provide the only adequate interpretation of life:

> . . . the structure of the classical Christian faith alone can satisfy the fullest and most stringent demands for knowledge. . . . The Christian revelation alone can provide the whole truth of life.[6]

Ferré looks to a time when the peoples of the earth will truly desire peace. Their motivation will come through "concerned commitment as response to reality, or love's commitment to meet as far as possible all human needs. . . ." The universal concern which is required must be rooted in "the very reality of God, man and all creation, and bearing the fruit of a viable, universal ethos."[7]

Thus, Ferré's theology appeals to the Christian revelation of God as perfect and sovereign love. Much of Ferré's writing endeavors to show how all knowledge and experience can be encompassed within this view. Reason alone cannot establish the reality of such a God, but neither can reason disprove it.

What distinguishes Ferré's position from some traditional supernaturalistic doctrines of God is not only the emphasis on *agape*, but the attempt to incorporate a dynamic-relational-evolutionary view of nature in a doctrine of God as supernatural personal Spirit. In this regard Ferré's thinking marks a forward step in the tradition of supernaturalism.

Obviously there is a great deal in Ferré's system of thought which must be taken "on faith." Some feel that he introduces unnecessary explanatory factors in accounting for things as they are. Still others find his approach to the problem of evil unsatisfactory. While Ferré makes many insightful comments on this problem, he insists that "without a future life, the Christian cannot solve the problem of evil. . . . Without life after death, we can find nothing but frustration of the highest human hopes."[8] Some critics of this logic insist that Ferré ultimately assigns the problem of evil to the mystery of the supernatural afterlife, but never gives an adequate accounting of how the fact of tragic evil can be reconciled with perfect, sovereign love.

God as Being-Itself

> God does not exist. He is being-itself beyond essence and existence. . . . The being of God cannot be understood as the existence of a being along-side others or above others. If God is *a* being he is subject to the cate-

> gories of finitude. Even if he is called the "highest being" . . . this situation is not changed . . . It is as atheistic to affirm the existence of God as it is to deny it. God is being-itself, not *a* being. . . . The statement that God is being-itself is a nonsymbolic statement. It does not point beyond itself. . . . However, after this has been said, nothing else can be said about God as God which is not symbolic.[9]

These words are likely to sound strange and bewildering to anyone who hears them for the first time. They were written by Paul Tillich, one of the most influential theologians of modern times. As a Christian theologian, Tillich was concerned with speaking meaningfully to the modern person. He adopted what he called the "method of correlation." According to this method, theology endeavors to correlate the ultimate questions which rise out of human existence with answers expressed in Christian symbols. "God," wrote Tillich, "is the answer to the question implied in human finitude."

Tillich does not come to the affirmation of the reality of God through arguments for God's existence ("God does not exist") nor by appeal to supernatural revelation. Rather, Tillich begins with the fact of existence. To exist as a human being is to participate in being-itself. Tillich follows what he calls the ontological way of coming to God—through being. God, then, is the presupposition of life, the "power of being in everything." Thus, God is not simply a segment of nature nor a being outside of nature. God is the depth and ground of nature, of all that exists. "He is the ground of the structure of being."

To be human, says Tillich, is to be anxious. Subject to fate and death, emptiness and meaninglessness, guilt and condemnation, finite man lives under the "threat of nonbeing." Man's experience is that of conflict and estrangement—estrangement from self, from other human beings, and ultimately from the very ground of life and meaning.

It is out of the threat of nonbeing and out of the experience of estrangement that the question of ultimate importance comes. It is "the question of a reality in which the self-estrangement of our existence is overcome, a reality of reconciliation and reunion, of creativity, meaning, and hope. We shall call such a reality the 'New Being.' "[10]

Tillich holds that the message of Christianity is the message of the New Being, manifest in Jesus as the Christ. In the picture of Jesus as the Christ we see one who participates in finitude but in whom the estrangements of finitude are overcome. There are no traces of estrangement between him and God. As one is grasped by the New Reality manifest in Jesus as the Christ, he is assured that being overcomes nonbeing. He participates in the New Being. He finds "the courage to be." Tillich writes, ". . . it was, and still is, this picture which mediates the transforming power of the New Being."[11]

To participate in the New Being is to accept one's acceptance; it is to affirm existence; it is to live in hope even in the midst of the difficulties inherent in the human situation. It is to participate in salvation, healing, wholeness.

Tillich's system of thought has been worked out in great detail. Our present concern is with his method of coming to the doctrine of God and the resultant God-concept. As we have seen, he comes to the concept of God as being-itself, or the ground of being through existence. To exist as a being is to participate in the power implicit in all being. The ground of being, he has written, means "the creative source of everything that has being." With this approach Tillich circumvents the traditional naturalistic-supernaturalistic argument. He denies "a world behind the world" or a supernatural Being. At the same time, he denies that God is to be identified with a segment of nature or with the sum total of things. Rather, God is the ground of all that has being. He goes on to indicate various symbolic ways of speaking of God: as living, as personal (although in actuality God is said to be suprapersonal), as love, as spirit.

Tillich is not original in holding that God is being-itself rather than *a* being. However, his particular formulation of this point of view has created much interest in our time and represents one of the contemporary attempts to point the way to an advance in theology by avoiding some of the logical and religious problems involved in referring to God as *a* being. Many persons have been helped through Tillich's writings to see that the life of faith may include honest doubt and searching. Faith does not stand or fall with traditional views of God as a supernatural being.

If Tillich's approach to the doctrine of God succeeds in circumventing some of the problems involved in thinking of God as *a* being, and also in traditional supernaturalism, it is not without difficulties of its own, both philosophical and religious. The concepts of being and nonbeing involve a vagueness of meaning. They throw little light on why things are the way they are; they provide little basis against which consequences can be checked; they fail adequately to communicate the dynamic, relational, evolutionary character of reality as we experience it and as we learn of it through investigation. As Charles Hartshorne and others have pointed out, the concept of *process-itself* might be more appropriate than being-itself. The need is for a doctrine of God which clarifies, more than does Tillich's, the nature of God's relationship to time and to changing events in the temporal process.

There is much of the neoplatonic mystical tradition in Tillich's thought. Salvation is ultimately a mystical reunion with the unchanging ground of being. There is a long and important religious tradition which is oriented to this approach. However, insofar as we are to think of the whole person in relation to the whole of reality, more consideration needs to be given to the values and meanings which emerge through relationship to the structures and processes involved in the more dynamic dimensions of existence. The notion of being needs to be balanced with the notion of becoming.

Another contemporary theologian whose doctrine of God has much in common with Tillich's is John Macquarrie. In his book *Principles of Christian Theology*, Macquarrie develops the concept of God as *holy being* in contrast to the idea of God as *a* being. Being is defined as "the act or state or condition of being. . . ."[12] Being refers to "the condition that there may be anything whatsoever." In the revealing situation, being is experienced as holy and/or gracious; thus Macquarrie speaks of God as *holy being*. Accordingly, being "is" not, but rather "lets be" in the sense of "enabling to be, empowering to be, or bringing into being."[13] The word "God," says Macquarrie, has a twofold meaning: "an ontological meaning, insofar as the word denotes being, and an existential meaning, insofar as it expresses an attitude of commitment to, or faith in being."[14] The divine characteristic of letting-be indicates the meaning of love: "helping a person into the full realization of his possibilities." The Christian is one who manifests the "letting-be of love" and so is brought into a closer relation with God. Man's ultimate hope, says Macquarrie, is in the God who has acted in Christ, the God who lets-be.

God as Transcendent Subject Known in the Faith-Event

Thus far we have considered two contemporary ways of affirming the reality of God. The first way, represented in the theology of Ferré, stresses knowledge of God as supernatural personal Spirit, given in supernatural revelation. The second way is that of Tillich in which God is affirmed as being-itself. The method of coming to this affirmation is existential and ontological, the personal experience of participating in being.

A third approach to the God-question and the affirmation of the reality of God is that of Rudolph Bultmann, distinguished German New Testament scholar and theologian. Bultmann insists that God is not an object to be investigated, nor a being whose reality is to be proved by argument. In fact, it is difficult to talk about God directly. The most meaningful speech about God is speech about man and human possibility. God is not so much an object to be investigated as he is a transcendent subject who addresses man. God encounters man in the world, in time, offering the possibility of a new existence. Man *may* make the decision of faith.

Drawing on the philosophy of the existentialist philosopher Martin Heidegger, Bultmann understands the human situation to be one of anxiety as man is continually subject to death. In his anxiety, finite man seeks security and meaning through reliance on tangible, material realities. In the process he falls into "inauthentic existence." Sin is man's attempt to achieve security and meaning through his own power and through tangible realities. Guilt is man's refusal to acknowledge and accept his finite, creaturely status.

The Christian gospel, according to Bultmann, is the good news of the possibility of authentic existence through faith in Jesus Christ, in whom God has overcome guilt and death. The authentic individual lives in the material world and uses it, but he does not permit it to determine his life. Through the faith-event, in encounter with God through Christ, man becomes free in a new way; he trusts in the grace of God; he is free from the world and free to be in the world in service to his fellowmen. He is free from the past and open to the future.

According to Bultmann, it is in the faith-event that man is able to speak meaningfully of God. Under these circumstances one does not speak of God in an abstract, detached sort of way. He speaks out of personal involvement as to what God has done and what God has given. He witnesses to the grace of God. Thus, meaningful affirmation of the reality of God is not an affirmation of the existence of a being somewhere. Rather, it is witness to a grace which has been experienced. It is impossible to speak meaningfully of God apart from personal faith-encounter-involvement:

> Christian faith believes that God acts upon us and addresses us in the specific here and now. This belief springs from an awareness of being addressed by the grace of God which confronts us in Jesus Christ. . . . This kind of faith . . . can only be an event occurring on specific occasions, and it can remain alive only when the believer is constantly asking himself what God is saying to him here and now. God is generally just as hidden for him as he is for everyone else. But from time to time the believer sees concrete happenings in the light of the word of grace which is addressed to him, and then faith can and ought to apprehend it as the act of God, even if its meaning is still enigmatic. . . . But still I must ask what he is trying to say to me . . . even if all he has to say is that I must just grin and bear it.[15]

There is a strongly subjective dimension to Bultmann's theological approach. One does not speak directly of God as an object; rather, the believer witnesses to the reality of freedom-in-faith which is accepted as a gift from God. To speak of God as Creator is not to affirm some theory of the beginning of the world; it is to understand oneself as the creature of God. To speak of God as Redeemer is to speak of the God-given possibility of a new, authentic existence.

Critics of Bultmann's position have held that his emphasis is so much upon the subjective dimension of the life of faith that the importance of actual, historical events is neglected and there is little room for speaking of God in an objective way. In response, Bultmann has said that to speak meaningfully of God's act must involve reference to an act in a real and objective sense. Nevertheless, it must be acknowledged that Bultmann has not come forth with a developed doctrine of God showing how God is related to the on-going eventfulness of the world.

Bultmann has long been concerned about the problem of communicating the Christian gospel to modern man who no longer believes in the supernaturalistic three-story universe. The Biblical cosmology is prescientific; it is mythical in character. Bultmann calls for a method of demythologizing through which one may come to the truth which is shrouded in the mythical New Testament setting. Myth should be interpreted existentially, so that the gospel message may be heard in relation to man's self-understanding as an anxious creature, existing inauthentically, but with the possibility, through Jesus Christ, of a new life.

Many modern persons have lost awareness of God, and faith in him, according to Bultmann, for two reasons. First, they have lost faith in the supernaturalism with which the God-idea has been traditionally associated. Second, they have lost faith because of the secularization of the world which involves "the world being conceived by man as an object and thus being delivered over to technology as its object." Thus, man loses the sense of life and the world as being received as a gift from a transcendent source. Bultmann refers to God as transcendent source (over against man) but without adopting traditional supernaturalism. God is acknowledged both as the transcendent over against man, and the God who is present with and for man. In God the dimensions of ultimacy and intimacy are united. Bultmann has little to say about what God *is*, let alone about the *existence* of God as being or as *a* being. Statements about God ultimately are based upon the experience of encounter with Jesus Christ and the new life in faith.

> Only the idea of God which can find, which can seek and find, *the unconditional in the conditional*, the beyond in the here, the transcendent in the present at hand, as possibility of encounter, is possible for modern man.
>
> It then remains to keep oneself open at any time *for the encounter with God in the world, in time*. . . . What is demanded is selflessness, not as a pattern of moral behavior, but as the readiness not to cling to ourselves, but to receive our authentic selves ever anew.[16]

A growing number of theologians, who have been influenced by existentialism, share the view that God is not an object to be investigated or whose existence is to be proved. Rather, they insist, one may speak of God indirectly by speaking of man and his possibilities. God is affirmed in the faith-event. Herbert Braun, for example, speaks of God not as one who exists for himself, but who is "the whence of my being agitated." He holds that man as man implies God.

This mode of thought serves in reminding us that religiously meaningful talk of God involves God's meaning for man. What is missing in this approach is clarity on the issue of God's relation to the inexorable structures and processes to which man is subject in the world in which he lives. The point of view we have been considering is vague in speaking to the question of how we may affirm meaningfully the reality of God as the Real-Other. It would also appear that on Bultmann's premises only the Christian can speak meaningfully of the reality of God.

God as Process and Structure

There are contemporary theologians who believe something of great importance is missing in the theologies we have discussed thus far. The missing factor is adequate attention to the processes and structures to which man is continually subject and which are decisively implicated in his existence.

It is the contention of these theologians that man must be understood as *a creature in context.* Man's arrival, survival, and growth in a meaningful existence can be understood only by taking his total environment into account. There are environmental structures, forces, and processes which are fundamental to man's very being and becoming. From this point of view, faith and hope are not imposed from without; they emerge in connection with man's response to and involvement in fundamental structures and processes. Revelation is not independent of the matrix in which it occurs.

It follows from this line of thinking that the search for God must move toward the basic processes and structures which are implicated in the coming of life and in the coming of faith and hope. Thus, whatever more God may be, God is at least the creative reality immanent in the processes and structures which so profoundly affect man. The theologians we are now to consider begin their inquiry about God, not by appealing to supernatural revelation (as does Ferré), nor by appealing to the fact of being (as does Tillich), nor by appealing exclusively to the faith-event and faith-possibility (as does Bultmann), but by appealing to *man in his cosmic context.* Both man and the context are perceived in dynamic, relational, and evolutionary terms. From the point of view we are now considering, man's hope for a meaningful existence is grounded in the cosmic whole of which he is a part, and more specifically in those processes and structures which are implicated in the coming of faith and hope. The reality of God is most meaningfully affirmed in relation to these processes and structures.

It is the contention of process-theologians that all meaningful talk of God presupposes some perception of the world in which God is present and in which God acts. It is their further contention that a dynamic-relational-evolutionary view of reality opens the door to a deepened understanding of how God is implicated in the processes of becoming. Such a view helps to bring together the conceptions of a dynamic, acting God with a dynamic universe. The door is opened to an understanding of time, process, and history as important to God.

Process theologians believe that traditional Christian imagery takes on deepened meaning in the light of a more dynamic view of God as immanent. The revealing person, the revealing-interpreting drama, and the witnessing-serving- reconciling community of faith all point to the ordering-creating-life-giving reality discernible in the fundamental processes and structures of the universe. Thus, the life of faith and hope, and the work of theology, are seen in close relation to the on-going processes of life and of the universe. Process theologians are convinced that their line of thinking opens the door to serious communication between theology and the various intellectual disciplines of our time, including the sciences.

There are important differences among process-theologians. Some of them (such as Henry Nelson Wieman) would apply the name "God" to a specific phase or aspect of the cosmic processes. Others (such as John Cobb and Schubert Ogden) draw heavily on the process philosophies of Alfred North Whitehead and Charles Hartshorne. However, these men go beyond Wieman's method in appealing to the witness of Christian experience and Biblical revelation. Wieman is essentially a philosophical theologian who frequently uses Christian symbols because of their power to express and communicate depth of meaning. Cobb and Ogden proceed from a more specifically Christian stance, seeking to relate the Christian understanding of God as love to the God disclosed in the fundamental processes and structures of reality. While their ultimate purpose has much in common with that of Ferré, they seek to avoid the logical difficulties which attend the supernaturalistic theism which Ferré espouses.

Henry Nelson Wieman, who for many years was associated with the University of Chicago, has long maintained that the only valid theology is one based on evidence derived from experience, interpreted by reason. Man's hope is grounded in realities to be found within the natural order—and there alone. Religion is basically commitment to the source of value or of human good. It has to do with man's orientation in the natural world; it is the quest for the greatest good possible for man.

The God-question, according to Wieman, is this: "What operates in human life with such character and power that it will transform man as he cannot transform himself, to save him from the depths of evil and endow him with the greatest good, provided that he give himself over to it with whatsoever completeness of self-giving is possible for him?"[17] Wieman goes on to say, "The word 'God' should refer to what actually operates to save and not merely to some belief *about* what operates in this way."[18]

Wieman contends that there is an operation in nature and in human relationships which issues in human transformation and the coming of value. This operation he calls "creative interchange" or "the creative event." Man is transformed, says Wieman, not through supernatural activity, but through participation in and commitment to a more-than-human working manifest in creative relationships.

Human life is transformed for the good, according to Wieman, through a process of reorganization. Persons are made new as they enter into such relations with each other that they participate imaginatively in the experience of the other, share meanings, grow in their appreciative perspectives, see life in terms of new possibilities for growth, and commit themselves in response to this vision of possibility. While persons may create conditions which are conducive to such transformation, creative-interchange is a more-than-human working. The same creative source which is manifest in the vast cosmic processes is present in creative human relationships. It is in commitment to this "source of human good" that man finds his highest meaning and hope. In his earlier books Wieman drew heavily on the thought of Whitehead in stressing the cosmic dimension of God's activity. In his later books he has spoken more specifically of God's activity in interpersonal relations.

Wieman reinterprets various Christian symbols in the light of his view of God as "creative interchange." The church is the fellowship in which creative interchange is dominant even as it was in the fellowship of Jesus. Salvation is deliverance from commitment to created things issuing in commitment to the divine source of value. Resurrection is the breaking of bounds which limit one's creative interchange to those of one's own cultural heritage; it is the coming of the capacity for interchange on more inclusive levels and thus participation in a fuller life.

Wieman insists that we may indeed affirm the reality of God—the God whose transforming power is manifest in creative relationships of giving and receiving. This God, says Wieman, is not a person but is superpersonal, creating and sustaining personality and bringing personality to its highest fulfillment. In an age in which man has the power to destroy himself, man's abiding hope is through devotion to the divine source of human good:

> This bomb has become a symbol giving to all human life a new meaning with portent of dread and splendor . . . It calls for a radical redirection of man's controlling devotion. . . . The creative source of value must come first in man's devotion. . . . This reversal in the direction of human devotion is not new. It is, we believe, the very substance of the original Christian faith. What is new is the need to reinterpret the creative source of human good in such wise as to render it accessible to the service of the mighty tools of science and technology.[19]

Although Wieman's theology has attracted considerable attention, it has been subject to criticism by numerous Christian theologians on several grounds: (1) It is said to be a philosophy of religion rather than a Christian theology grounded in the revelation of God in Christ; (2) it is said to give inadequate place to the personal dimension of God's being; (3) it is said to limit the scope of God's activity to the level or sphere of interpersonal relations; (4) it is said to provide little basis for a life of personal devotion and worship. Wieman has responded to all of these criticisms, expressing the conviction that if new ground is to be broken in theology it must be along the lines he has suggested.

Among contemporary theologians there are a number who insist on the importance of speaking of God as an objective reality, and who believe that process philosophy (as developed by Alfred North Whitehead and Charles Hartshorne) provides an important resource for the theologian. They would go beyond Wieman in their appeal to the Christian revelation of God in Christ and in their insistence that God's reality is best understood in personal terms. At the same time, they would deny that God is unchanging, perfect substance. On the contrary, God is vitally implicated in the changes of the world and is affected by the relationships in which he shares. John Cobb and Schubert Ogden are representatives of this theological approach.

Cobb holds that there is a distinctive mode of existence made possible by God's work in Jesus Christ. A Christian natural theology is required (1) to help the Christian better to understand what it means to affirm the work of God in Christ, and (2) to enable the Christian to carry on meaningful conversation with the person who makes no faith commitment. In his book *A Christian Natural Theology*, Cobb develops a conception of God on the model of "a living person"—omnispatial, "the reason *that* each new occasion becomes," the ground of being, purpose, and order. Cobb implies that a knowledge of God's presence and agency in the world at large illuminates the work of God in Jesus Christ.

Ogden approaches his discussion of the reality of God against the background of a deep interest in the philosophical theology of Charles Hartshorne and the demythologizing method of Rudolph Bultmann. His concern is to find a conception of God's reality which overcomes what he regards as the inadequacies of traditional supernaturalistic theism. It is his conviction that it is in the context of our shared experience as secular men that God's reality can be affirmed with meaning.

The key to Ogden's understanding of the God-idea is found in this statement:

> I hold that the primary use of "God" is to refer to the objective ground in reality itself of our ineradicable confidence in the worth of our existence. It lies in the nature of this basic confidence to affirm that the real whole of which we experience ourselves to be parts is such as to be worthy of, and thus to evoke, this very confidence. The word "God", then, provides the designation for whatever it is about this experienced whole that calls forth and justifies our original and inescapable trust. . . .[20]

Following Hartshorne, Ogden holds that God "is to be conceived in strict analogy with the human self or person." Using this analogy in the context of process-thought, Ogden reinterprets the meaning of God as love, creator, redeemer, the God who acts in history, the God whose reality is re-presented in Jesus Christ.

The trend of thought among the more recent process theologians represents a dual concern: (1) to witness to the Christian vision of God in Jesus Christ; (2) to show how this vision illuminates the human situation at the same time that our newer perceptions of reality in terms of process illuminate the nature of God's involvement in the world. The hope which is set forth in this type of Christian thought is not that of an eventual fulfillment of all needs and desires in another world. Rather, it is the possibility of a new mode of authentic existence in a world in which being and becoming, life and death, are wondrously interrelated and in which the living God is vitally involved.

Experience and the Affirmation of God's Reality

The ground we have covered in this chapter indicates that serious theological work is being done in our time. There are theologians who are coming to grips with the varied challenges to traditional conceptions of God and traditional views of man and the universe. If there is no clear consensus on many theological issues, there is a shared conviction among the theologians we have discussed that the God-question is of vital importance, and that we need to seek new ways of affirming God's reality.

It is significant that a growing number of theologians insist that meaningful talk about God must have some identifiable relationship to man's experience. A crucial difference between the humanist and the person of religious faith is found at this point. The humanist insists that he finds nothing in his experience which speaks of the reality of God or which calls forth faith in God. The person of religious faith, however, asserts that there is that in his experience which witnesses to the reality of God. Contemporary theology endeavors to indicate where on the map of human experience discourse about God has a meaningful place.

Most Christian theologians insist that the most meaningful talk about God proceeds from what God has done through Jesus Christ in revelation and in the bringing of a new life of faith. Theology on this level is largely confessional in character, articulating what is given in Christian experience. Such theology may deepen the Christian's own self-understanding. The non-Christian may be interested to hear what the Christian has to say and what his experience leads him to believe about God. Indeed, the Christian's vision *may* inspire the non-Christian to some new vision of God.

However, the non-Christian is justified in saying to the Christian, "I do not share your vision of God. I have not come to participate in a new life of faith, hope, and love through Jesus Christ. Does this mean that I am excluded from meaningful talk about God?"

This is a question of great importance. Is there that in our experience as *human beings* which speaks of the reality of God? Is there that in the world about us which in some sense declares the reality of God? In other words, can we affirm the reality of God not only from the stance of Christian faith, but also from the stance of human beings in a world about which we are learning more and more? In Chapter One we insisted that the whole person asks the question of God by virtue of his humanity. Can we now go on to say that out of human existence itself we may meaningfully affirm the reality of God?

13.
Toward a Theology of Hoping

IN THE PRECEDING chapter we saw that contemporary theologians follow differing routes in formulating the God-idea and God-question, in affirming the reality of God, and in formulating concepts and images of God. It is not surprising that there should be differences of opinion in matters of such complexity and importance. This is no time for dogmatism in theological matters. It *is* a good time for recognizing the importance of the God-question, for clarifying the various possible approaches to it, and for pursuing the various approaches as carefully as possible so that we may see the implications and possibilities in each approach.

In this chapter we shall move toward still another way of affirming the reality of God. It is related to concerns and convictions shared by process theologians. However, it differs from the approach of some of the process theologians in associating God with the wholeness of reality rather than with some abstracted phase or function of reality or with some "entity" or "being." It recognizes the need for utilizing models and analogies in speaking of God, but insists that no one model or analogy can stand alone in providing viable God language.

This chapter is intended to present some first steps toward formulating a theology of hope and hoping. It will appeal primarily to the universal need for hope and the processes by which persons come to a life of faith and hope. In Chapter Fourteen we shall deal more fully with the concept of God in relation to the wholeness of reality. In Chapter Fifteen we shall consider more specifically the Christian experience of hope and its implications for the affirmation of God's reality.

Some Underlying Convictions

Fundamental to the particular affirmation of God's reality to be developed in this book are several underlying convictions. They are presented in summary fashion with a minimum of elaboration:

1. Man lives by hope. The human creature comes alive in his hoping and dies a spiritual death in his despairing. There is a measure of hope and of hopelessness in each of us. The particular form or content of appropriate hope varies from situation to situation. What is required is at least enough hoping to enable one to function with a reasonable degree of satisfaction and efficiency. Hope involves expectation. It has to do with the feeling that there is possibility in one's situation. It involves the readiness to take the next step and to meet the new day. Hope sometimes involves a desire for specific goals and the anticipation that they will be achieved. Sometimes hope is an undefined expectancy, an openness to what lies ahead in the conviction that there is worth in living and that reality is ever in the making.

2. Mature religion involves man's orientation to the whole of reality in hope. At the heart of life is the hunger for expression and fulfillment. The religious vision provides man's most enduring hope when man is frustrated in his yearning. It pro-

vides a perspective on life in its farthest reaches, setting the whole range of human experience in an order of meaning. Although immature forms of religion are outgrown, the religious vision and perspective is of abiding importance, undergirding human life with morale and motivation.

3. The word "God" has its primary meaning in the framework of religious life and thought. The God-idea is the idea of an ultimate, objective ground of faith and hope. The God-idea suggests a reality on which man can count when all other grounds of security and meaning collapse or disappear. God is the object and ground of religious faith, devotion, and hope. The crucial God-question is: "In what sense, if any, can we meaningfully affirm that there is that in or about reality which corresponds to the God-idea?"

4. The quest for an answer to the God-question leads to a search for understanding of the nature of man himself, his relationships, and his most inclusive physical, psychological, social, and cosmic environments. It leads to the search for fuller understanding of all that is implicated in man's being, becoming, and hoping. Whatever more God may be, God is the ground of man's being, becoming, and hoping. This means that the search for God cannot be carried on in abstraction from a study of the matrix in which man lives and moves and has his being. God is to be discerned in relationship to those conditions, structures, and processes implicated in man's being, becoming, and hoping. The reality of God has to do with what John Dewey called "the matrix of our being and the inescapable condition of our lives."

5. The theory of reality and the doctrine of God presented in the remainder of this book presupposes an organismic theory of personality. The individual person is best understood as a total, functioning unit in dynamic and reciprocal relationships. This theory assumes that the human organism is not a dual system of mind and body. On the contrary, it is a single reality

consisting of many part-functions. Each individual person is a center of thinking, feeling, aspiring in dynamic context. Man is an integral part of the natural order, unique in his capacities for self-transcendence and situation-transcendence.

6. The model or analogy of organism can fruitfully be extended to the wider ranges of reality. The world order is not simply a collection of separate events or bits of matter moving about in otherwise empty space. The most fruitful analogy for interpreting the world order is not a machine, but an organism in which the parts and the whole are interrelated and interdependent. Reality is dynamic, relational, evolutionary, holistic. The perception of reality as organic process or patterned process combines a recognition of the uniqueness of each individual with a recognition of the interdependence of the parts and the whole. This view overcomes the sharp dualisms of nature and supernature, material and spiritual. At the same time, it is sympathetic to the concept of levels and dimensions and diversity within the fullness of reality.

7. In the light of an organismic view of reality, including man, the door is opened to a reinterpretation of the concepts of immanence and transcendence. The concept of immanence (to dwell in or to be present in) suggests the interrelatedness of all things; nothing exists in isolation or in self-sufficiency. The concept of transcendence (to surpass or go beyond) suggests the dimension of more-than-ness. The whole is more than any one part; it is more than the sum total of the parts; the concept of "a whole" combines the notions of immanence and transcendence.

One of the most meaningful words in our vocabulary is that of "community." Whether or not one is aware of living in and belonging to a community makes a profound difference in his self-image and in what life means to him. A community, like all wholes, is real and intangible at the same time. The community-reality is immanent in the parts (persons, institutions, and so on) but also transcendent to them. Where the sense of community goes deep, persons celebrate the values and meanings attendant upon their community-life with varied symbols, rituals, and festivals. The vision of community puts things in a different light and enables the individual to recognize himself in relation to an ongoing significant reality. The word "God" begins to take on experiential meaning when we recognize it as a verbal symbol pointing to *the ultimate community of meaning to which man belongs*—the ultimate community of meaning in its being, becoming, and deepest character. In this sense God is both immanent and transcendent in relation to the particular events of the world.

8. The God-idea is the idea of the Ultimate-Real-Other experienced as faith and hope conferring. The idea of ultimacy has to do with what we keep coming to or what we are continually up against in all times and experiences. In his Ingersoll lecture on immortality, Alfred North Whitehead spoke of God as "the intangible fact at the base of finite existence." If there is indeed a ground of hope which transcends immediate facts and values and loyalties, it must exhibit the dimension of ultimacy. It has to do with a fact "at the base of finite existence."

9. Intellectual integrity requires that we recognize the inevitability of living with vast mystery and ignorance. Some persons may speak with finality about their personal feelings or convictions, but no person is in a position to speak with finality about the reality of God. We must leave the door open to many possibilities. Specific philosophies, world-views, and God-concepts may serve fruitful functions in organizing data and in articulating perceptions of how things are. They may express convictions and feelings and evoke various responses. But their functional significance needs to be recognized, along with the possibility that new knowledge and deeper experience may necessitate fundamental reconstructions in philosophical and theological thought. Thus, no finality is claimed

for the point of view developed in the remainder of this book. What is intended is a formulation of a possible way of affirming the reality of God. There will not be the formulation of a well-rounded and complete doctrine of God, but rather a pointing to a dimension of the God-reality which is neglected in much contemporary theological discussion.

10. The approach to the God-question being set forth involves the conviction that all forms of experience must be given a hearing in the search for the truth of how things are, including questions concerning the reality of God. Sense experience, introspection, feelings of derivation and relatedness, religious experience, antireligious experience, a-religious experience all need to be taken into account and subjected to critical analysis and evaluation. The data of experience are what we have to work with, but all experience is subject to critical analysis and no one experience can be regarded as providing the whole of truth. A person may claim that he has come to the ultimate truth of things through a particular event or experience. It is his privilege to hold this conviction. It is not his privilege to expect other persons to accept his conclusions apart from attention to all kinds of experience and the application of serious principles of reflective understanding. The testimony of the religious person that his experience indicates the presence of a Real-Other providing strength and hope is important testimony. It may inspire and encourage others. However, its truth value for other persons involves the application of tests of truth just as surely as would be required in reference to other truth claims.

11. Any meaningful affirmation of the reality of God involves a demonstration of the relevance of the God-idea in human experience. The thesis of this chapter is that the primary meaning of the God-idea for man is in the experience of hope and hoping, with particular reference to this experience within the limitations to which man is subject. Inquiry concerning

the reality of God, therefore, leads to inquiry into the factors involved in the coming and maintenance of hope.

Marks of the Hoping Person

The difference between hoping and despairing is the difference between inner life and inner death of the spirit. The hoping person exhibits a readiness for the next step, a movement toward what might be but is not yet. He exhibits the quality of wakefulness, as though living in expectation of the not-yet. Whereas the person of despair lives with a sense of being trapped, the person of hope feels that somehow there is a way out and that there is the potentiality for meaning in his situation. Sometimes it involves little more than hope for some kind of change in one's situation, or of deliverance from what seems to be an intolerable condition. Sometimes it involves the hope for power to endure what seems unendurable. Sometimes it involves much more, but in all instances hope involves an openness to the future with a measure of expectancy. The person of hope is able to wait, not simply in defeat or resignation, but in anticipation. The acid test of hope is met in the presence of life's limiting and frustrating situations including disappointment, loss, suffering, and death. However, hope has to do with one's total life-orientation and is manifest in the way in which an individual approaches each new situation and each new day.

The hoping person exhibits the capacity for wishing.[1] He has not settled back into a life-style of apathy or boredom. He cares about some things, and out of his caring come wishes of his own. The hoping person has enough emotional investment in living and enough will-for-meaning that he wishes for what might be.

The hoping person exhibits the capacity to relate—to his

own wishes, to other persons in a giving and receiving way, to reality factors in his situation, to causes, to goals. The capacity to relate is a matter of degree and may vary from situation to situation, but it is always a component of hope. The despairing person, on the other hand, is out of touch. His mechanisms of relating may have broken down. He experiences the pain of ultimate loneliness, the feeling that he is not and cannot be meaningfully related.

The hoping person exhibits the capacity for imagination. He is able to work in terms of images, possibilities, or hypotheses to be tried out. The imaging-work of the hoping person may involve a belief-system and/or a theory as to how things are and might be. The hoping person has perceptions of himself, other people, life-situations, and sometimes of reality in its more inclusive ranges which come to be expressed in images. Healthful hoping involves images which tend to unite fact and value and aspiration, without recourse to the building of fictional worlds.

Finally, the person who hopes in a sustained and healthful way exhibits enough inner flexibility and resilience of spirit to be able to go along with the inexorable changes in life. He is able to adjust to the closing and opening of doors of opportunity. He is able to change direction in "the middle of a play" if this is indicated. He is able to find meaning in situations which provide only partial realization of his dreams and expectations. The hoping person maintains a zest for living in circumstances that are less than ideal.

Thus, the foundations of hope lie partly within the human being himself. Hope emerges in the interplay or interaction of the person with his more immediate situations and with his more inclusive environment. It is not only in the component factors in one's life-situation, but in the interplay of the factors and in the situation in its wholeness that we must seek the wonder of the coming of hope.

Prerequisites for Sustained Hope

Research into the dynamics of hope and hoping is complicated by the fact that persons respond so differently to similar circumstances. A situation which is utterly demoralizing to one individual may be highly challenging and stimulating to another. Obviously, personal and internal factors are involved. We are learning more about what they are, but we need to know much more than we do about the factors and processes involved in the coming of healthful and sustained hope. Significant progress has been made in understanding physical and psychological factors which are involved. As indicated earlier, the foundations of hope lie partly within the individual.

On the other hand, it appears that if hope is to be sustained through changing circumstances, if hope is in some sense to be undergirded by factors beyond man himself, we ought to be able to point to certain prerequisites for hope in the nature of the way things are. Hopes based on illusions are doomed to die. We may be sustained for a time by fantasies, but sooner or later we must come to terms with stubborn facts. Hope requires more than the determination to be hopeful.

If we had some guarantee that everything is going to turn out happily we would have the required external basis for hope. However, we have no such guarantee, despite the fact that some people seem to think that it is the function of religion to provide it. There is nothing in presently available knowledge and experience to guarantee that everything is going to come out happily. Tragedy is a fact. Under these circumstances hope must seek another kind of grounding. In addition to man's own capacity for decision, certain conditions in reality would seem to be required if hope is to be justified. These conditions presumably would provide the *possibility* for the coming of meaning and value without necessarily guaranteeing their coming. What would such conditions be?

At a minimum level, hope requires three conditions in the individual's total situation: a measure of dependability, change, and the possibility of the coming of the new. Without these, there is no hope for going beyond the status quo. Without some dependability and order, man's situation would be chaotic. Without some change and the possibility of the coming of the new, things would always be at a standstill. So long as a person has reason to believe that his situation is within a matrix of some dependability, so long as he has reason to believe that his situation is subject to change, so long as he believes there is the possibility of the coming of the new, there is a basis for hope in fact.

The grounds for a justified hope are greatly strengthened when two further conditions obtain: a measure of responsiveness in man's larger environment and the presence of a value-conserving process. It makes a profound difference in one's hoping if there is reason to believe that there is that in his cosmic environment which responds to his efforts, which in some sense accepts him and grants him permission to go on from where he is. It makes a profound difference in one's hoping if there is reason to believe that there is something cumulative in the cosmic processes, and that along with the loss inherent in the temporal processes something of value is nevertheless conserved.

There is a ground for hope in the belief that whereas one cannot erase all the past nor save all the past, he can go beyond the past, outgrow it, and carry with him some meanings out of it. A universe exhibiting dependability, change, the coming of the new, a measure of responsiveness, and value-conservation would be a universe *potential for meaning and hope.*

There are thinkers who are convinced that this is precisely the kind of universe in which man's life has come into being. In various ways Samuel Alexander, C. Lloyd Morgan, Jan Smuts, Alfred North Whitehead, Charles Hartshorne, Teilhard de

Chardin and others have set forth this cosmological perspective. Sir James Jeans, the astronomer, wrote:

> The old physics showed us a universe which looked more like a prison than a dwelling place. The new physics shows us a universe which looks as though it might conceivably form a suitable dwelling place for free men and not merely a shelter for brutes—a home in which it may at least be possible for us to live . . . lives of endeavor and achievement.[2]

The process philosophers and theologians have integrated this perspective in their systems of thought. We shall return to this theme in considering the idea of God in relation to the wholeness of reality. This mode of thought opens the door to a theology of hoping which is grounded in the nature of man and in the nature of the inclusive scheme of things of which man is a part.

14.
God and the Wholeness of Reality

IN CHAPTER THREE, religion was referred to as "that way of life in which man finds his ultimate hope in God." Like many other human beings, the religious person finds hope in relationship to *persons* (family, friends, associates, identification-figures, persons of influence and power in whom he has come to trust) and through *causes* with which he has identified himself. Hope is relational; it is attached to something or someone. Such hope as most of us have is related directly or indirectly to persons and causes.

The person of religious orientation sees his significant persons and causes in relation to a still more ultimate and inclusive frame of reference. The God-idea, as we have seen, suggests a dimension of ultimacy; it suggests that which one keeps coming to and that which one is up against in all experiences and relationships. The person of religious faith and hope not only lives toward what he believes and feels to be ultimate reality, he responds to this reality in trust, devotion, and hope. He is sustained in the conviction that in life and death one is never really alone. He shares with all other creatures a relationship to what is central and enduring in the nature of things.

The Conviction of Dealing With a Real-Other

"Whoever I am, Thou knowest, O God, I am thine!" Thus wrote Dietrich Bonhoeffer from prison. In this statement he expressed the fundamental and persistent element in religious faith—the conviction that in life and death, in good fortune and ill-fortune, one is dealing with the Sacred-Real-Other. The confidence that one's ultimate relationship is with a Divine Reality is at the heart of the faith of the more mature religions.

The deepest religious conviction is grounded in experience. The person of first-hand faith points to that in his experience which he is convinced cannot be accounted for simply in terms of human resources. The fundamental sense of the worth of life, the sense of having received life, the sense of the holy, the conviction of being judged and called into question, the experience of a sustaining, saving, delivering good after one's own efforts have proved fruitless, the sense of being called or summoned, are among the experiences to which religious persons point in affirming the reality of the Divine-Real-Other. To the question, "What calls forth this deep feeling of the worth of life, the sense of the holy, the awareness of being called into question, the experience of peace, forgiveness, assurance, and hope and the sense of being summoned and claimed?" the person of religious faith replies in effect, "God."

The humanist says that he finds nothing in his experience which speaks of God. The person of religious faith replies that he can only speak for himself, but in his experience he *does* find that which speaks of the Divine-Real-Other. He may speak in terms of divine power or divine presence or divine purpose or divine love. In these and other ways he affirms his conviction that in the midst of life he is dealing with a dimension of transcendence, a reality beyond all particulars and more than the sum total of particular things.

The history of religions displays the amazing diversity of

ways in which through the years people have conceptualized the Divine-Real-Other in which they have believed. They have used the intellectual and linguistic tools which were available to them. Often these tools have involved questionable intellectual presuppositions. Many God-concepts have reflected belief in the supernatural conceived in other-worldly terms. The only way of affirming the reality of the divine, transcendent Other seemed to be in the language of supernaturalism, other-worldliness, miracle.

It is this supernaturalistic way of talking about God which is proving to be such a stumbling block to many persons today. The humanist may say, "There is nothing in my experience which speaks of anything more ultimate than man and society and a physical universe." There are others, not able to accept traditional supernaturalism, who nevertheless believe and feel "I do indeed experience intimations of a dimension of ultimacy and transcendence, a sense of something more than things which can be perceived and measured, call it what we will—the infinite, the transcendent, God." Such persons choose to be loyal to the idea of God even when the actuality of God is mystery.

There is no way of proving that the experiences to which the person of faith appeals are not illusory or that they cannot be accounted for on physiological-biological-psychological-sociological grounds. It is very difficult, however, to convince the person of religious faith that this is the way it is. His deepest persuasion is that in his personal life, and in his life within the community of faith, he deals with a divine reality. The most eloquent affirmation of the religious person's conviction of the reality of God comes in his continuing to hope even when human resources are spent and in an ultimate sense he is "up against it." Specific concepts of God come and go. The fact of hoping persists, even at the limits of human strength and life. This is the clearest affirmation of the conviction of the reality of God. As indicated in Chapter Twelve, a number of contemporary theologians have endeavored to formulate doctrines of God which take seriously the data of the religious life as well as contemporary understandings of man, society, and the universe. While these attempts have met with mixed responses, enough has been done to demonstrate that there are significant alternatives to traditional supernaturalistic theism. The deeper persuasions which attend the life of faith are not rendered meaningless by the passing of prescientific modes of thought or by linguistic analysis.

In what follows, we are proposing to take seriously the conviction of the person of faith that he is dealing with a Real Other, the ultimate source of his hope. In this exploring nothing will be "proved." But out of it may come a way of seeing things which make sense to at least some people, which helps to put experience in some sort of meaningful order, which illuminates the religious life, and which provides a basis for recognizing oneself and the human venture in relation to an inclusive frame of orientation and devotion.

The Reality of Parts and Wholes

When a person is lost it is not simply because he does not know where he is; in a sense, he knows this. His larger problem is that he does not know where the rest of the world is. To lose one's bearing is to be out of touch with some larger reality of which one is a part. To know who and what and where one is, is to experience oneself in relation to some structure or pattern or community of events. To be alive as a human being is to have a place in relation to other persons and places.

Reality in its deepest nature is social in character. Nothing exists in complete isolation. Persons, things, events are unique in their individuality, but they possess no individuality apart from their involvement with other persons, things, and events.

To talk about reality is to talk about persons, things, and events in relationship. The social character of reality is manifest on all levels—whether we are dealing with electrons, atoms, molecules, cells, organs, organisms, groups, communities, societies, or epochs of history.

The fundamental interrelatedness of things leads us to think of reality in terms of parts and wholes. It is highly significant that in virtually every modern investigative field the perception of reality in terms of parts and wholes is being pursued and is proving to be fruitful. The physical scientist deals with systems as well as with components. The biologist finds relevance in the concept of organism. The psychologist seeks an understanding of the whole personality structure of the individual. The social scientist seeks to understand man in a social matrix. The anthropologist studies a culture as an integrally functioning system. And so we might go on. Individuality, plurality, interrelatedness, and the dimension of wholeness all apparently are involved in the way things are.

Through many years, some people have believed in a philosophy of reductionism—everything can be reduced to its constituent parts. The adequacy of this view is now seriously questioned. Persons, objects, events, component things are indeed real, but today they are thought of as real in relationship, in their involvement in some more inclusive whole or pattern or structure of events. To understand how things are, we must understand that parts influence wholes and wholes influence parts. Neither exists in isolation nor abstraction. In the vastness and complexity of reality many levels of activity and organization are discernible, but the social character of reality is manifest on all levels.

We have previously indicated that today man increasingly thinks of reality in dynamic, relational, evolutionary terms. If now we add to this perception the part-whole way of seeing things, the door is opened to a new day in man's understanding of himself and his world. The static, deterministic categories seem strangely out of place. The drawing of sharp and absolute distinctions between body and mind, matter and spirit, being and becoming, fact and value seem inappropriate. The amazing interplay of events, organizations, and processes reveals an exciting scheme of things, with possibilities for good and evil, creation and destruction. Our experience indicates that this is the way things are.

Contemporary investigations indicate that there is a dimension of order in the universe. At the same time, there appears to be a dimension of randomness. We can predict some things on some levels with a high degree of probability. But we cannot predict everything. This is what we might expect in a dynamic, relational, pluralistic, evolutionary scheme of things displaying parts and wholes in conjunction. The universe does not appear to be a closed and completely determined system of events.

There are important implications for theology in the contemporary ways of understanding man and his universe. Static, other-worldly categories need to be replaced with categories and symbols that point to process, relatedness, becoming, and the dimension of wholeness. It will be an exciting day in the religious world when more persons are able to rethink basic doctrines in the light of newer, more dynamic perceptions of reality.

To speak of wholes raises the question as to whether there is some final, all-inclusive whole with definable characteristics. The only answer at this time is: We do not know. But there is good reason to believe in the reality of wholes, and of that which is fundamental to the emergence of wholes. There seems to be a holistic dimension of reality and in this sense we may speak of the wholeness of reality. It is this concept of "the wholeness of reality" which suggests a way of talking about God.

God as the Wholeness-Reality

What we keep coming to in all experiences—what we finally are up against in our living and dying—is not simply a single event or experience or thing or function or entity. It is reality in its diversity and wholeness. In man's arriving, surviving, and departing he is subject to a highly complex and dynamic scheme of things, involving many relationships, processes, and structures. There are some persons who believe that back of all this there is a single power which originates and in some measure orders this scheme of things. The truth of such a belief can neither be verified nor falsified.

The person of religion tends to think of what he is finally up against in terms of some sort of unity; he is convinced of the reality of the Divine-Real-Other. Monotheistic religions insist that God is One. Insofar as the person of monotheistic faith attaches trust, devotion, and hope to this One, it is appropriate that he should use the word God. As we have seen, this is a religious term and can most appropriately be used in the context of religious response and discourse.

The fact that the religious person tends to think of the object of his trust and hope in terms of unity should not obscure the fact that in his living and dying man deals with a multiplicity of factors. He deals with parts and wholes. He lives in an encompassing matrix and in a course of events. Even as he deals with particular persons and situations he also participates in a dynamic continuum within which individual entities emerge, continue with changes for a time, and eventually pass on. Therefore, if one uses the word "God," he ought to use it in the understanding that the ultimate reality man is always coming up to combines unity and diversity, wholeness and particularity, immanence and transcendence.

The concept of wholeness does not imply a static, completed structure of some sort, nor does it necessarily imply "all there is." It refers to reality in its related diversity and eventfulness, in its amazing interplay of parts, dimensions, levels, and wholes. It refers to that character of reality by virtue of which all parts of the known universe are sensitive to all other parts and are mutually affected by each other. Reality manifests a sensitized relatedness of the parts, and in this sense is a functional whole. By virtue of this functional wholeness, it is appropriate to speak of entities "passing on" or "passing to" or "passing into" rather than "passing away." To exist as an individual is to contribute to the whole of which the individual is a part. It is in the matrix of patterned process that we live and move and have our being.

A certain vagueness and imprecision inevitably attend the word "wholeness." We prefer words which point to the concrete, the specific, the tangible, and the measurable. However, it is our preoccupation with the concrete, specific, and tangible which gets us into so much of our difficulty as human beings. Creative living also involves attention to another dimension of reality. It is a dimension which gathers up such elusive realities as sources, relations, patterns, potentialities, qualities, and goals. The word "wholeness" functions in pointing to the dimension of comprehensiveness. It refers both to the totality and the part-whole structure of reality.

To live in the light of the wholeness of reality is to see things in a different way. Matthew Arnold reminded us that to see life steadily is to see it whole. At the point where we begin to see a person in the light of his origins, backgrounds, relationships, interests, and potentialities we begin to see him in a clearer light. We see him more fully and more truly.

The concept of wholeness suggests reality in its depth and breadth and height; in its being and becoming; in its vastness and intensity; in its potentialities and qualitative richness; in its never-ending interplay of persons, events, and situations; in its creation, disintegration, and re-creation; in its flux and in its long-range dependabilities; in its impartiality and integrity; in its endings and new beginnings; in its mysterious uniting of fate and freedom, tragedy and triumph, death and life, creation and redemption. Realistic and enduring hope is ultimately grounded not in some segment of reality, but in the character of reality in its wholeness.

The hypothesis being suggested, then, is that we think of God not as an isolated being or process or function, but as the Wholeness-Reality, experienced in trust, devotion, and hope. In this perspective, God is not a being "out there," or a mysterious being-itself "down there," or a feeling of process "in there," or an event "back there." Rather, God may be spoken of variously as *the ground of wholeness, the character of reality in its wholeness, the dynamic reality making for wholeness.*

What the complete or ultimate nature of God may be we do not know. We can think of many possibilities, but the full truth of the reality of God eludes us. We must seek an appropriate style of life with partial knowledge. However, we are in a position to bring such knowledge and experience as we have to the greatest question of all, the God-question. We can witness to such light as is ours, speaking in varied languages, reflecting varied perspectives.

We know more than we once did about the structures and processes involved in the universe and in man's arriving, surviving, becoming, and hoping. We know something of what it means to be a whole person in relation to the whole of reality. If God is vitally involved in these matters, we presumably can say something about where and how God is experienced and something of the character of God's working. The hypothesis being presented here is that whatever more God may be, God is the Wholeness-Reality fundamental to the universe in its dynamic, relational, evolutionary fullness and open-endedness, and fundamentally implicated in man's arriving, surviving, becoming, dying, and hoping. If God is not implicated in these matters one may well question the meaningfulness of talk about God.

To speak of God as the Wholeness-Reality is to affirm the transcendent dimension of reality without falling into other-worldly supernaturalism. The ideas of immanence and transcendence are held in tension and correlation.

In this holistic approach, power and value, process and structure, limitation and potentiality, integration and disintegration, part and whole, life and death are held together in *patterned process* by virtue of the reality of God. Recognition is given to the hopes and meanings which are potential in relationships and in networks of association. The fundamental movement of reality relevant to the life of man, in this view, is a movement toward wholeness of linkages. It is consistent with this approach to conceive of God as the integrity of reality, the power of being and becoming, implicated in all events and experienced as "the intangible fact at the base of finite existence."

Conceiving of God in a Different Way

The proposal that we think of God as the Wholeness-Reality may strike many persons as strange. We are so accustomed to associating the God-idea with a first cause or a supreme ruler acting from the outside that it is difficult to think of God as the very heart and ground and organizing center of reality in its complex and ever-moving fullness. However, this is not really a new way of thinking; it is a particular way of thinking in the present day under new conditions, with new knowledge available to us.

For many centuries there have been theologians and philosophers who have been deeply impressed with the dynamic and interrelated character of all things. They have recognized that an adequate accounting must go beyond a tabulation of the parts. On the other hand, they have not been satisfied with talking simply about an external agent or about a fixed, final, static, substantial whole in which the parts were really swallowed up. Many attempts have been made to express the *more-than-the-parts dimension of reality*. However, it has not been until relatively recent times (with the coming of dynamic-relational-evolutionary views of nature, man, society, reality) that we have been in a position to make much progress in this attempt. Over forty years ago Jan Smuts moved in the direction of this type of thinking in his book *Holism and Evolution:*

> Both matter and life consist of unit structures whose ordered grouping produces natural wholes which we call bodies or organisms. This character of "wholeness" meets us everywhere and points to something fundamental in the universe. Holism is the term here coined for this fundamental factor operative towards the creation of wholes in the universe. . . . As Holism is a process of creative synthesis, the resulting wholes are not static but dynamic, evolutionary, creative.[1]

Among the writers in this century who have endeavored to relate this kind of thinking to the God-idea is Harry Overstreet, who defined God as "the everlasting creative life that moves toward wholeness."[2] Relatively few attempts have been made to utilize the resources of this way of thinking in serious theological work. There has been resistance to theologies which were suspected of being "too naturalistic." However, with growing understanding of scientific methods, and with newer insights into the "nature of nature," there is a new openness to theologies which incorporate a contemporary "theology of nature." Modern man increasingly understands himself to be a whole creature (not body and mind in separation) in a whole universe combining unity and diversity.

While there will probably always be those persons who

will feel more comfortable with traditional dualistic categories, there are many others who are convinced that new experiences and new understandings call for more dynamic, relational, evolutionary, holistic categories. To speak of God as the Wholeness-Reality is to take a step in moving in this direction in theological thought. It is to recognize that organic and inorganic, matter and spirit are related. It is to recognize that the coming of life, meaning, idealism, faith, hope, and wholeness is inextricably interwoven with processes variously understood in physical, biological, psychological, sociological, philosophical, and religious terms. It is to recognize that man is part of a web of being, and that to see life truly is to seek it in its particularity and in its wholeness. *What man is continually dealing with and coming up against in his living and dying is not a blank wall, but a reality of dynamic wholeness, of going forth, of creativity and potentiality.*

There are two points of crucial importance at which the concept of God as the Wholeness-Reality differs from many God-concepts. First, as developed here, God is not understood as being a guarantor that specific things are going to happen or that all situations are going to come out in a certain way. Rather, God provides the *conditions* by virtue of which there are *possibilities* (as well as limitations) in situations. By virtue of the reality of God, there is the possibility of meanng and hope for man in a given situation, but there is no guarantee that he will realize it or that events will turn out happily.

A second difference between the idea of God as the Wholeness-Reality as discussed here and some other ideas of God is found in the *locus* of hope and expectation.

Traditional religious views have frequently looked for hope outside the world and outside the changing events of experience. Deliverance from limitations and change has been sought. The suggestion is here being made that we need to orient our living and aspiring in line with the fundamental character and movement of things as they are—in their relatedness, interplay, and becoming. Life in this age cannot be organized productively around the static and the other-worldly. We need to seek orientation and guidance in the context of our existence, in the discernment of long-range dependabilities and directions, in patterns of process and behavior which are disclosed in the nature of life itself. This approach may lead to chastened expectations, and to a reconsideration of what constitutes appropriate human hoping. On the other hand, it will nurture expectations more in harmony with the fundamental structures and processes of reality as experienced. In this view, the hope which God makes possible is not a hope *despite* the limitations inherent in existence, but *through* these limitations.

The image of God as the Wholeness-Reality draws no sharp line between sacred and secular. The secular is sacred in its wholeness. The image of God as the Wholeness-Reality recognizes that at the heart of life, and supremely in man, is the persistent urge for expression and fulfillment. Life is for living; in the depths of our existence we know it and seek it. And if life is worth living, it is worth living well.

The deepest resources for significant living are not encountered by turning from the pain and wonder of responsible existence-in-relationship. They are encountered in recognizing the relational character of all existence and in seeking such growth in and toward wholeness as is possible. Life itself mediates courage for living. God is where the whole-making, whole-seeking is. Life is holy in its wholeness.

In the next chapter we shall look further into the idea of God as the Wholeness-Reality. We shall endeavor to relate this way of thinking to several more familiar ways of speaking of God.

15.

God as Ground, Grace, and Goal

THE ISSUE of despairing and hoping is at the center of human existence. The decisive element which often tips the scales in the delicate balance of despair and hope is the vision of reality by which one lives. How one perceives what is ultimate in the nature of things and how one perceives his relationship to the Ultimate-Real-Other is the factor which makes the crucial difference in determining the nature of one's hoping and despairing.

In earlier chapters we have asserted that hoping is the distinctive characteristic of the religious response to life. The God-idea, it was said, is the idea of an ultimate, objective ground of faith and hope. The crucial God-question was said to be: In what sense, if any, can we affirm that there is that in or about reality which corresponds to the God-idea? In the preceding chapter, the hypothesis was advanced that we may indeed affirm the reality of God in the context of a vision of reality as dynamic, relational, evolutionary, holistic—displaying an ultimate relatedness of parts and wholes. More specifically, it was suggested, we may appropriately speak of God as the Wholeness-Reality.

The purpose of this chapter is to speak further of what is designated in speaking of God as the Wholeness-Reality, and to indicate what illumination this concept of God brings to the age-old question of human despairing and hoping.

The Condition We Cannot Escape

> No man is an island entire of itself. Every man is a piece of the continent, a piece of the main. If a clod be washed away by the sea, Europe is the less. . . . Any man's death diminishes me, because I am involved in mankind. Therefore, never send to know for whom the bell tolls. It tolls for thee.

In these words John Donne pointed to a condition of cosmic scope we cannot escape: in its deepest nature, reality is relational. No fact stands alone. No person, object, or event exists by and of itself. The identity, behavior, and meaning of any reality can be understood only in relationship to some pattern, configuration, community, or whole of which it is a part.

To be a person is to be a center of thinking, feeling, valuing, and aspiring. It is to be uniquely oneself. It is to experience the sense of being in a world of one's own. But it is also to experience the sense of being related—to past and future, to other persons, to an encompassing whole. The sense of "otherness" may be dimly apprehended, but it is there. Sometimes it is experienced as a sense of dependence; sometimes, as a sense of being mystically related to a "more"; sometimes, as a sense of being acted on; sometimes, as a sense of duty. Thus, the experience of being alive as a human being is a dipolar experience; uniqueness and relatedness are conjoined. Man is born for both solitude and belonging. His experience exemplifies the part-whole, relational character of reality.

There is mounting evidence that human life realizes its finest possibilities as it moves toward wholeness of linkages. The life of the individual person moves toward fulfillment in relationships. To adopt a life-style of self-sufficiency, exploitation, cruelty, or irrationality is to move against the nature of reality. The pattern of health and well-being for the human person is a pattern of movement toward wholeness of life in relation to the whole of being. Man's experience on the human level points to the inescapable condition of reality on all known levels—reality is relational.

Thus, his experience in its totality indicates that man is continually dealing with a reality of ultimate importance conjoining the integrity of the individual with the integrity of the whole. This reality is the ground of wholeness and the dynamic reality making for wholeness. It is the Wholeness-Reality.

As man comes to recognize the Wholeness-Reality as the very ground and source of his being, the reality which defines the fundamental limitations, conditions, and possibilities of his existence, the reality which calls forth in him the sense of worth in living and evokes a response of reverence, trust, hope, and commitment, he affirms the reality of God in his total being. Even as the whole person asks the question of God, so the whole person affirms the reality of God.

God and Our Ultimate Concern

To speak of God is to speak of what concerns us ultimately. Our ultimate concern has to do with *existence in hope*. We appropriately use the name "God" to designate the ultimate ground of hope of which we have knowledge and to which our experience witnesses. It is in this understanding that we have affirmed the reality of God as the Wholeness-Reality. The ultimate ground of hope of which we have knowledge is the dynamic reality of cosmic dimensions making for wholeness.

In order to justify naming the wholeness-reality concept "God," several conditions must be fulfilled. It must be shown how the hypothetical wholeness-reality does have basis in fact. This we have endeavored to do. It must be shown that the wholeness-reality concept can and does function in providing a frame of orientation in terms of which the data of experience can be coherently organized and reinterpreted in hopeful perspective. It must be shown that this concept illuminates the data of religious experience. It must be shown how this concept nurtures hopes, expectations, and a life-style appropriate to the cosmic context in which man lives and moves and has his being. It must be shown how this concept can function effectively in providing a rationale for the life of devotion and for rites of passage from one significant life experience to another in which attendant values are recognized and celebrated. Mature God-concepts function in these various ways in the religious life. In this and succeeding chapters the attempt will be made to relate the wholeness-reality concept to these various functions.

The Testimony of Religious Experience

It is conceivable that a person with no particular religious interest might reflect on the human situation, the relation of parts and wholes, the fundamental structures and processes of reality, and out of it all come to the concept of a wholeness-reality. But it might never occur to him to call this reality "God." What, then, is the difference, if any, between the wholeness-reality concept in the context of philosophical speculation and in a religious approach when the reality of God is affirmed as the Wholeness-Reality?

Historically, both philosophy and religion have been interested in gaining knowledge about the world. Religion's ultimate concern, however, has not been the gaining of knowledge for the sake of knowledge. Religion is concerned with the quality of man's life and with his relation to the whole of being. The person of religious concern asks the God-question not simply out of intellectual curiosity. He asks the God-question from the perspective of deep concern for the finding of faith and hope and meaning in his existence. Thus, the person of religious concern would not ask simply if it is meaningful to talk about a wholeness-reality as a philosophical concept. He would ask whether such a concept is meaningful in the context of religious concerns and aspirations and experiences.

The deepest convictions of the reality of God are based on experience. Probably the spiritual pilgrimages of no two persons are identical; there is a private dimension to the God-man relationship. Nevertheless, affirmations of the reality of God have a way of coming back again and again to some form of witness to the personal experience of God as sustaining presence, transforming power, life-giving purpose, redeeming love. In his book *The Idea of the Holy,* Rudolph Otto wrote about the experiential basis of religious conviction. It was his conclusion that the feeling of awe in response to what is experienced as the Holy *(mysterium tremendum)* is at the center of religious experience and of the conviction of God's reality. Various writers interpret religious experience differently, but there is widespread agreement that the deepest conviction of the reality of God is usually based on what is believed to be the personal experience of God. Insofar as the solution of a difficult problem attends the experience, the conviction is deepened. Thus, the person of religious faith is convinced that in life and death he is dealing with a Divine-Real-Other.

In considering the concept of God as the Wholeness-Reality, it may be illuminating to give attention to three widely-reported dimensions of religious experience. God, it is often reported, is experienced as the *source or ground* of all that has being, including human life. Again, it is affirmed that God is experienced as *saving grace*, whereby man is helped, forgiven, delivered from some distressing condition, made whole. Again, it is affirmed that God is experienced as *goal*, the end and final purpose of man's existence. Thus, God is experienced as the ultimate reality with which man deals. Various concepts of God have been formulated and utilized in providing theological interpretations of the experience of the Ultimate-Real-Other as ground, grace, and goal.

God as Source or Ground of Being

One of the important functions of the God-concept is in helping man to identify himself in relation to the "supreme context in which he rightly belongs" or to the whole of which he is a part. In fulfilling this function, God-concepts usually involve some theory of man's coming into being; of the conditions which are fundamental to his situation, to which he is subject, and by which he is judged; of the values most worthy of man's supreme devotion; of a way or style of life witnessing to man's commitment to God. God-concepts on this level not only purport to state certain matters of fact but also to interpret the deep conviction of the religious person that life is given to him, that he is dependent on a Real-Other for life and continuing life, that the basic conditions of life are determined by the Divine-Real-Other, and that man lives under a continuing judgment.

The concept of God as the Wholeness-Reality opens the door to a way of understanding man's place in the universe which draws upon insights from science, philosophy, and theology. This concept is related to a contemporary interpretation of the doctrine of creation.

A credible doctrine of creation recognizes that there are persistent questions about the beginning of the world and questions as to why things are the way they are for which we do not have answers. Man has no way of knowing about a creation out of nothing nor of an originating reason for the existence of the world. The question "Why is there a world at all?" is a meaningful question, but for man it is an unanswerable question. Neither science nor theology can speak with finality on this issue. Dietrich Bonhoeffer described the human situation when he wrote, "Man no longer lives in the beginning—he has lost the beginning. Now he finds he is in the middle, knowing neither the end nor the beginning, and yet knowing that he is in the middle, coming from the beginning and going toward the end."[1]

Despite the fact that much mystery attends the human situation, there are highly important clues and guidelines for the living of the significant life in hope. We can speak meaningfully of the reality of God as creator, even though we cannot speak with assurance about an absolute beginning. A contemporary doctrine of creation affirms the dependence of the world on God, the goodness and potentiality of creation, the giftlike character of life by virtue of which man is called into a responsible existence in relation to the Creator. A meaningful and hopeful life for man is undergirded by such an understanding of the doctrine of creation.

To speak of God as the Wholeness-Reality is to acknowledge God's creative activity to be continuous. There is a continuing coming-into-being in the universe. Man's arrival, survival, and becoming are related to the coming-into-being processes which are cosmic in scope. Human fulfillment comes through participation in the divine, creative work which is continuous.

It is given man to know something about how the divine creative work proceeds. New insights have come in the modern period by way of new concepts of causation. The single-cause, linear theories of causation have been called into question. Causation is now understood as involving a context of many factors and events. For every effect there is a field of relational factors. Reality is forever shaping itself out of the interplay of forces. Every event affects and is affected by the activity of the universe.

The appearance of water may be used to illustrate a contemporary understanding of the contextual and relational character of creativity. Man does not account for the appearance of water by a single push from an external agent. Man accounts for the appearance of water by synthesizing processes involving hydrogen and oxygen in a dynamic matrix of events. The evolutionary processes bring forth what Teilhard de Chardin called "creatures of syntheses." Even though man does not know whether the universe had a beginning (a "unique creation") or whether the universe is a perpetual motion machine, we do know something about the processes of creative organization and creative interchange through which new realities come into being. On all levels reality exhibits the coming of new wholes which are more than the sum of constituent parts. The creative dimension of reality brings forth the genuinely new. Ian G. Barbour writes:

> Each human being, for example, is truly a new creation, and every poem, painting, or symphony is a novel event which cannot be completely accounted for by its past. Creation is not just the rearrangement of the given, but the origination of the genuinely new. Yet creativity always works in what exists to bring into being what did not exist.[2]

The creative processes which have produced man are part of a vast, cosmic evolutionary order involving creation and destruction, integration and disintegration, life and death, feeding into each other. The universe appears to be unfinished and open-ended, involving trial and error, randomness and order. Nevertheless, a fundamental dependability and impartiality are discernible in the cosmic wholeness. The rain falls on the just and the unjust. There are basic conditions which cannot be violated without resultant suffering and destruction. These conditions are fundamental to the coming of life and to human well-being. In learning to live in harmony with the fundamental character, structures, and processes of reality man moves toward fulfillment as a human being.

Even though randomness and atomic indeterminacy are part of the cosmic story, an overall direction of development can be discerned with trends toward increasing complexity, versatility, and individualization. Thus, the universe in which man dwells exhibits a dimension of reality which transcends or is more than the tangible and measurable—a dimension of order, dependability, integrity, directionality, creativity, wholeness, and whole-making. It is this dimension of reality to which we point when we speak of God.

It is for man to find a way of life or life-style which is appropriate to his own nature and to the larger reality of which he is a part. It is usually futile to try to raise plants, flowers, or trees in the high mountains if their natural habitat is in the lowlands. The principle involved is relevant on the human level. Man lives with both possibilities and limitations. He needs to take both into account in his hoping and expecting. Many years ago, the philosopher Boethius pointed out that many of man's troubles are the "penalty of mistaken expectations." The dignity of man involves his capacity to see himself in relation to the creative, whole-making life of the universe. Even though man must live within the limitations inherent in human finitude, he has the capacity for participating in a unique way in the fulfillment of the cosmic drama. To grow toward wholeness as a human being through the varied experiences of life is to share in the glory of creation.

The character of reality encourages a life-style of searching, experimenting, reaching after the unattained. The cosmic conditions under which man lives are not conducive to the prediction of final results with certainty. But the conditions are excellent for venturing forth, striving after goals, for the winning of a sense of integrity and worth through the linking of life with life, through work and play and creative effort. Persons may appropriately hope to grow toward fullness of experience in moving toward wholeness of linkages. Life can have cumulative meaning through intensification of significant relationships.

Creation and re-creation cannot be separated—and therein lies further hope for man. Because creation is continuous, no single event or experience can be counted as final. When losses have been sustained and things seem to have gone to pieces, there is a basis for hope in the provision for creative reorganization of life. Time is real. It is the nature of reality to move beyond the past. While the past cannot be erased, it can be transcended and related to the present and future in new ways. By virtue of the creative-re-creative dimension of reality, man is enabled to keep alive the expectant attitude, knowing that even in the midst of loss elements from the past are gathered into new chapters of reality.

It is as man awakens to the wonder of the wholeness of which he is a part, and as he responds in trust and commitment to the challenge and claim with which he is confronted, that the reality of God breaks in upon him. Often some creative event comes to have illuminating, revelatory significance. Reality in its wholeness is discerned in its depth, profundity, sanctity. Thus, God is not experienced simply as an object "out there" or as a "feeling inside." God *comes*, God *appears*. God *is present*. Many theological questions may still be unanswered, but the person of faith is convinced that any adequate accounting of reality must reckon with an Ultimate-Real-Other putting all existence in a different light. It is in the vision of the Ultimate-Real-Other as the source of existence, and in the attendant response of trust and commitment, that the wholeness-reality of philosophical speculation becomes for man the Wholeness-Reality of religious devotion.

Thus, the vision of God as the Wholeness-Reality, the source, condition, and ground of being, enables man to see the varied elements of experience in a structure of relatedness, to seek goals appropriate to his own capacities and situations, to maintain a hope born of the creative-recreative reality at the heart of life. Philip H. Phenix has written:

> To know the world profoundly, in its origins, actualities, possibilities, and promises, is to know God, and to live in the world with unconditional concern for the realization of its manifold and multiform excellences is to worship him in spirit and in truth.[3]

God as Grace

The testimony of religious experience is not only that God gives life and provides the underlying conditions in terms of which life is to be lived, but God also graciously gives himself, doing for man what man cannot do for himself. Thus, religiously adequate God-concepts not only provide the structural ideas for a comprehensive belief system, putting experience into an ordered pattern; they also identify the caring, sustaining, help-conferring, saving realities in man's total situation. This is what is implied when we say that in the life of religion reality is experienced *as gracious*. God is experienced not only as source and ground of being, but also as grace.

The recurrent testimony of the religious life is that by

virtue of the grace of God despair is turned to hope. Through God's grace men are given power to endure, forgiveness, moral ennoblement, nutriment for the spiritual life, a new relationship with self and man and God, a sustaining and inspiring awareness of God's presence, a living joy and hope in the face of life's most threatening experiences.

In a theology affirming the reality of God as the Wholeness-Reality, there is a frank acknowledgment that there is much we do not know about what God *is* or even *how* God is. Nevertheless, there is much of importance we can say about where and how God is experienced, how God works, how man may appropriate divine grace, how man may relate to God.

In the theological perspective of which we are now speaking, the grace of God is believed to be mediated in and through relationships. Life-giving grace is not understood as an infused potency or favor arbitrarily bestowed by an external God. Rather, grace is the power for being and becoming more whole, appropriated in the midst of life, as man is open to the deep resources mediated in work and play and love and worship and commitment to the God who is ever working in events toward greater wholeness. What man is continually meeting in his living and dying, in his succeeding and failing, is not a blank wall, but a reality of dynamic wholeness, of going forth, of creation and re-creation, of potentiality. In relationship to such a reality there is hope for new beginnings.

To speak of God as source is to speak of that reality by virtue of which new entities and events come into being. To speak of God as grace is to speak of that dimension of God's working by virtue of which that which has been estranged, broken, and counted evil is accepted and gathered into a new structure of wholeness and meaning. Such words as healing, reconciliation, forgiveness, redemption suggest the experience of God as grace.

In the world of nature we see the wondrous working by

which healing takes place. We see that which has been expelled by one form of life as useless being utilized by other forms of life for survival and growth. On the human level, we observe redemptive processes by which situations counted hopeless or evil issue in new structures of hope and worth. Thus, there is a redemptive dimension of reality at work on all levels of existence.

Just as the concept of God as the Wholeness-Reality illuminates the creative processes by which man comes into being, so the concept of God as the Wholeness-Reality illuminates the processes by which man is enabled to go beyond loss, tragedy, and estrangement into a new existence. Fundamental to the redemptive processes of life is the divine working by virtue of which parts are gathered into wholes and what seems useless by itself takes on significance in relationships. The reality which makes for wholeness is a caring, sustaining, healing reality, the ultimate ground of human hope.

If God is indeed the reality manifest in the work of creation, re-creation, and whole-making, then we may reasonably expect to encounter God in a great variety of places. Indeed, God is encountered in all events and situations and relationships where barriers to wholeness are being broken down and life is being freed for growth, expression, and fulfillment. The grace of God is sometimes manifest in difficult situations where men go forth to help persons in need, to witness for justice and human dignity, to work sacrificially for social structures conducive to the enhancement of human welfare. The divine redemptive processes are not only present within the individual and in person-to-person relationships. They are present in social processes by which despair is turned to hope, enslavement of the spirit is turned to a new life of dignity.

Human life finds an important part of its fulfillment through participation in the gracious, redemptive work of God. Man appropriates divine grace in being open to resources continually being offered him and also by seeking to be an instrument of grace. On the human level, God requires the vision, purpose, and work of man in carrying on the work of whole-making. Man himself is called to be a mediator of divine grace in human relationships.

In a familiar Old Testament story, Jacob is described waking from a dream and saying, "Surely the Lord is in this place; and I did not know it" (Genesis 28:16). Men continue to be surprised in experiencing the grace of God in unexpected places and ways. Sometimes man is surprised in the grace that comes to him. Sometimes he is surprised in the way he himself is used as an instrument of grace for others.

God as Goal

Persons of religious faith frequently testify that beyond their experience of God as ground and grace, they experience God as the Real-Other who lays claim on the life of man, summons him into service, and leads him toward and into a destiny beyond the here and now. Thus, God is experienced as goal. Life is fulfilled as man moves toward and meets in faith the God who comes to him.

Here again it is the task of theology to provide theological interpretation of what is given in experience. The holistic theology being developed in this book recognizes that it is the nature of life to seek expression and fulfillment. Man, by nature, is an aspiring creature. The meaning of human life is not only in finding and arriving, but in seeking and aspiring. In this sense, destiny is continually in process of being fulfilled.

However, there is more to be said. The meaning of man's existence is to be found through actualization and self-realization *in relation to the whole of which he is a part.* Reality in its wholeness involves the dimension of potentiality. God as the Wholeness-Reality is forever acting as a lure upon man, seeking to draw him out of isolation and self-centeredness toward greater wholeness of being. The pattern of health, well-being, and hope for man is grounded in the pattern of reality in its movement toward wholeness. To seek the comfort and complacency of the static is to exist in contradiction to the nature of reality. Man cannot know of one far-off goal toward which all creation moves, but he can discern a purposefulness inherent in reality—to bring forth the possibilities in persons and events, moving on toward wholeness of linkages. The destiny of man is fulfilled in relation to this purposiveness. God is encountered not only in the past and future, but in any and all situations where life is struggling for integrity and meaning. The life of faith and hope is born as men respond in such situations to God as the Wholeness-Reality, committing their lives in trust and service, seeking to be instruments of wholeness.

He who has been grasped by the vision of God as the Wholeness-Reality seeks God, not simply that he might be protected, consoled, or given a pleasant feeling, but that he might grow in likeness to God. This is the highest worship—to seek to grow into the likeness of the God who is experienced as the ground of being, as healing grace, and as the lure into greater wholeness of being. To translate this worship into life is not only to move toward personal fulfillment, it is to contribute to those with whom we are related; it is to contribute to wholeness in God. This is the road to whatever fulfillment there may be beyond the present sight of man.

16.
God and the Christian Experience of Hope

THE CHRISTIAN message is good news of hope in the midst of the pain and wonder of human existence. When the message is heard and received as being true, it comes as light on the human condition, as grace in the human situation, as possibility for a new existence of wholeness and meaning, and as summons into a life of discovery, growth, and service in the world. It comes as a message of deliverance from enslavement to self, to things, and to external circumstance into the joyous freedom to trust and hope and love in God.

The Christian message is grounded in faith in the God who acts throughout the cosmos, in human history, in human relationships, and in the souls of men—the God experienced as ground, grace, and goal. The earliest Christians were of Jewish background. Their understanding of God was rooted in their history. They believed in the creator-God who entered into a personal bond of covenant with his chosen people at Sinai and who promised deliverance to his people through the coming Messiah. It was their conviction that God had now acted decisively in Jesus Christ, putting past history in a new light, offering man a living hope for deliverance from sin and death and entrance into a new, victorious life empowered by the Holy Spirit.

To understand the meaning of Christianity for a devout Christian, it is essential to understand what is meant by revelation through historical events. Christianity does not begin with a general theory about the nature of reality. It begins with historical events as remembered—supremely the event of Jesus in relationship to those about him. The earliest Christians believed that God is known, not primarily through the speculations of the mind, but through actions and events. God, it was believed, had acted in entering into covenant with Israel at Sinai. Now he had acted supremely and graciously in the life, death, and resurrection of Jesus, who was the Christ because he was the fulfiller and transformer of Israel's expectations. The early Christians thought not simply that Jesus was one who brought teachings about the possibility of a new life through a relationship to God; rather, they believed that in him that new relationship and new life were actually realized. Thus, to be in Christ was to be a new creature *now*. Paul wrote, ". . . if anyone is in Christ, he is a new creation; the old has passed away, behold, the new has come. . . . All this is from God . . ." (II CORINTHIANS 5:17, 18).

The early Christians shared their new life in fellowship with other Christians. To be in Christ, Paul said, was to be the body of Christ. In this way the apostle used the analogy of an organism to speak of the communal dimension of the new life. For nineteen centuries Christians have used this analogy. Thus, from the beginning Christianity has united the concepts of individual and community—the part and the whole—in Christian experience. The community of faith is a community of shared memories and shared hopes. It is the Christian faith that through the community of faith God's gracious gift of new life is offered to man and mediated to him. Thus the community of faith is a group in covenant with God called to "declare the wonderful deeds of him who called you out of darkness into his marvelous light" (I PETER 2:9).

As indicated in Chapter Ten, the testimony of Christian experience is that Christian faith, hope, and new life come through and in association with the revealing person and the witnessing-serving-reconciling community of faith. In giving more formal expression to their vision and faith, Christians have used the language of doctrine. At the same time, they have used the language of drama—discerning God's revealing presence in various events set forth in a cosmic drama of creation and redemption. This drama is acted out in ritual and expressed in art, music, symbol, and sacred literature. The ultimate meaning of the drama is that God is involved in the world and in human life, providing the possibility of a new life of genuine maturity and fulfillment in relation to the whole of being. Thus, in varied languages the Christian community affirms its abiding faith that God's final word to man is one of grace and hope.

Fundamental to the Christian faith and way of life is the vision of God seeking to bring wholeness to man, in his inner life and in his relations with other men and with God. The God of Christian faith is a God whose creative power is declared in nature, whose redeeming love is made known in Christ, and whose active presence and summons to witness and service is experienced in his living Spirit. It is the Christian claim that the Christian vision illuminates the human situation with intelligibility, meaning, and hope. To walk in faith in the light of this vision is to walk in dignity and in the freedom to trust and hope and love. It is to be more whole as persons in relation to the whole of being. It is to be "more than conquerors" in the face of the most devastating experiences in human life. It is to be hopefully responsive to the challenges life presents.

The Contemporary Failure to Hear the Christian Message

Wonderful as the Christian vision and hope are, and profound as the impact of the Christian movement is and has been, the fact is that multitudes of persons do not hear the Christian message as being good news for them. In a day of competing faiths and philosophies, the Christian faith is having a difficult time being heard and accepted. There are those who say that even in the United States we are living in a post-Christian era.

Among the factors which appear to be operative in this situation there are four which seem to be particularly relevant: (1) the perspectives and values which are inherent in the Christian faith and way of life run counter to much in contemporary comfort-oriented cultures; (2) the Christian vision and hope are often obscured by theologies which fail to present a contemporary interpretation of the message; (3) the Christian vision and hope are often not understood because of the use of languages which fail to communicate; (4) the Christian vision and hope are often distrusted because of the frequent failure of organized churches to be witnessing-serving-reconciling communities of faith. It is repeatedly asserted that instead of communicating a message of new life and wholeness for all men in both word and deed, the churches often become fellowships of the withdrawn, the complacent, the unconcerned, and the reactionary. As one skeptic put it, "God may not be dead, but he seems to have left the churches."

In Chapter Nine the question was raised as to whether, in fact, there are important resources in the Christian faith for modern man as he seeks a faith by which to live in the twentieth century. We come now to an affirmative response to that question as representing the perspective of this book.

In the midst of destructive cleavages in man and society, there is a search for a vision of wholeness capable of calling forth the strengths and loyalties of men. In the midst of affluence and poverty, conflicts which lay waste the most precious of human resources, and profound loneliness in the souls of men, there is need for an encompassing and luring vision disclosing that to which men ultimately belong and by which they are claimed.

Christianity points to such a vision. Central to the Christian message is the affirmation of a transcendent reality bringing to man a word of judgment, of grace, and of hope. At this juncture of human history, when the destiny of man is being called into question, all significant voices that speak of hope need to be heard and measured. It is important that the Christian message be heard in its contemporary relevance. But this requires that continuing theological work be done along with continuing effort to translate the vision into deed.

Toward a Recovery of the Vision

Some of the most important insights bearing on the doctrine of God are now coming out of studies concerning man. To some persons this may seem like a strange and even paradoxical statement. But there is a case to be made for it.

We are learning much about the conditions and processes involved in human becoming and maturing. We are learning that there are recognizable patterns of human health as well as of human illness. To grow toward fullness of being as a human person is to experience the sustaining intimacy of the infant-mother relationship. But it is also to move beyond this relationship. In matehood and parenthood are possibilities for intimacy in the context of adulthood and maturity. The need for intimate belonging persists, but movement toward wholeness of linkages requires emancipation from infantile dependence. Growth toward health-in-humanness involves still another form of relationship—a *sharing* relationship with persons of mutual concerns. Obviously there are different kinds of sharing and different kinds of concerns manifest in such varied settings as home, school, church, office, shop, factory, laboratory, playing field, club, community projects, and so on. To share with other persons in significant interests and in dealing with significant problems on a *side-by-side basis* is to participate in the adventure of discovery; insights are gained about self, other persons, and the world. One's world becomes larger and qualitatively richer.

Growth into wholeness also involves the capacity for relationships-in-solitude. To be able to be alone without being lonely, to have a growing inner life of thought, discovery, appreciation, and searching is a part of being fully alive as a human being. Man is born for both solitude and belonging, for uniqueness and relatedness.

Living faith is born out of significant relationships, realized fulfillment and meaning, achievement through struggle, the experience of going beyond disappointment and tragedy, participation in new patterns of meaning woven out of the pieces of a broken past. *The fundamental direction of human life is toward participation in widening and deepening relationships of wholeness.* Through such participation comes fullness of life.

The truth of these statements is being verified not only through more technical studies but in the experiences of persons in daily living. Life is grounded in conditions and processes which provide the basic terms on which fulfillment of life is possible.

It is the genius of the Christian vision to disclose the ultimate reality through which life comes into being and in which the finest possibilities of life are realized. Christianity, as we have seen, speaks in the varied languages of doctrine, drama, poetry, art, myth, symbol, and ritual—but underneath them all is the affirmation that life is fulfilled in relationships of integrity and caring, learning, serving, and loving. The law is fulfilled, we have been told, in love of God and of neighbor. Again, it has been taught that the more excellent way of life is a way of faith and hope and love. Still again it is affirmed that the "fruit of the Spirit is love, joy, peace, patience, kindness, goodness, faithfulness, gentleness, self-control . . ." (GALATIANS 5:22-23). According to Christian faith, the more excellent way of life is grounded in what is central and enduring in reality. This life is supported and sustained by the deepest power in the universe. God, according to Christian faith, is a reality-not-ourselves making for creation and re-creation, reconciliation and wholeness. The distinctively Christian way of affirming all this is to say that God is love.

Attendant upon the Christian vision of God is the vision of personhood at its finest. To express this vision, the Christian faith sometimes uses the model of "maturity." The whole person, the person most deeply related to God and man, is the mature person. One of the important Biblical passages employing this model is found in the fourth chapter of the letter to the Ephesians where Christians are called to "mature manhood, to the measure of stature of the fullness of Christ." Christians are "to grow up in every way into him who is the head, into Christ" (EPHESIANS 4:15).

The Christian message issues in the glad proclamation of a hope and possibility for man—the possibility of a new life in which the accepting, forgiving love of God when received in faith releases man to accept himself, to affirm his own existence in dignity, to relate to other human beings creatively, to walk courageously in the assurance of God's presence, to work and serve in the world in gladness of heart, and to face the ultimate mysteries of life in the serene confidence that "whether we live or whether we die, we are the Lord's" (ROMANS 14:8).

It may be that in a time when many persons are skeptical

about traditional approaches to belief in God, our most immediate need is to talk to each other as fellow human beings concerning the life most worth seeking. It may be that out of such communication among men of goodwill there will emerge a growing awareness that human fulfillment comes in relationship to one another and to a reality at the heart of existence which supports and moves toward wholeness. We have been referring to this ultimate ground of fulfillment as the Wholeness-Reality.

It may be that out of such communication among men of goodwill there will emerge a growing and shared insight into a life in which persons understand that they have a right to be themselves; that while it is not possible to erase the past, they are permitted to outgrow the past; that the justification of life is in life itself as it is linked sensitively, courageously, and lovingly with other life; that in the midst of the deaths and rebirths man experiences throughout his days, he is contributing to a wholeness which can be glimpsed only in part, but which gives his life a significance greater than he knows.

To catch a vision of such a life, and to commit oneself to it, is to affirm the reality of God—the underlying condition or character by virtue of which life is fulfilled in the maturity of wholeness. It may be that to recover the Christian vision of life's wonder and hope in our time it will be necessary to be less concerned about justifying and interpreting old symbols, and more concerned about understanding the fundamental conditions, structures, and processes by which life comes into being, grows, and is fulfilled. There is reason to believe that such probing of life itself brings forth understandings which coalesce with the deeper insights of Christian faith. Life in its wholeness yields the vision of God.

What Christian faith claims as revelation is not independent of or contrary to the continuing revelations which life itself yields. On the contrary, Christian faith in its contemporary forms appeals both to the testimony of the investigative disciplines and to the testimony of revealing events—supremely the events associated with Jesus Christ and the community of faith which grew up around him. Daniel Day Williams has written:

> To speak of revelation in the prophets and in Christ is not to speak then of some supernatural doctrine added to our human knowledge from an extrahistorical source. It is to speak of those happenings in human history which have so opened our eyes, and so transformed our minds that the disclosure of God to man has taken place.[1]

The Christian affirms that in the revealing events of his community's history his eyes are opened to the creating, redeeming, whole-making reality of God. The truth which is given in reason and experience is not denied. It is now seen in the dimension of ultimacy. It is discerned in a light which illuminates the human venture with meaning and which calls man to glad commitment of life.

Thus, Christian faith in its highest forms articulates and celebrates the vision of God which life in its wholeness provides and sustains. It keeps pointing to the revealing person in whom the light of the Wholeness-Reality breaks forth again and again. It invites men into the witnessing-serving-reconciling community of faith which mediates the grace of God where men are struggling for hope and meaning, a community celebrating the drama of creation, redemption, and new life through worship, ritual, study, witness, and service. In varied languages the Christian faith affirms the reality of God whose highest worship is in a life of integrity, moving through the varied experiences of life toward wholeness, expressing the joy of being alive as an instrument of wholeness in the world.

Unfortunately, the world does not always see or hear

Christian faith in its highest forms. The fact that persons who take the name of Christian sometimes invoke their faith in support of attitudes, policies, and practices which separate, alienate, and dehumanize men indicates how tragically the vision of wholeness and love has been missed. How to declare the reality of the God of love is the greatest challenge facing Christianity today.

The God of Love and Human Maturity

> Beloved, let us love one another; for love is of God, and he who loves is born of God and knows God. . . . No man has ever seen God; if we love one another, God abides in us and his love is perfected in us (I JOHN 4: 7, 12).

Christianity has been referred to as the religion of love. According to its doctrine, God is a God of love who in mercy accepts, forgives, and brings man to newness of life. Man, in turn, is called to love of God, and in that love finds fulfillment.

Obviously, the interpretation of love becomes a crucial matter for an understanding of Christian faith.

The love of God is sometimes misinterpreted to mean that by virtue of this love man will be protected from danger, and that all man's goals and desires which have not been attained or fulfilled in this world will be attained and fulfilled in another world. The love of God expressed in terms of a parent-child model is sometimes interpreted to imply that throughout life a loving relation to God is one of absolute dependence. Unfortunately, immature dependencies are sometimes encouraged in the name of Christian faith. Again, God's love is sometimes interpreted primarily in terms of emotion or sentiment, or as favoritism toward a given group or race or nation. Such interpretations of divine love may be psychologically understandable, but they are theologically irresponsible.

If God is most truly known as acting creatively and redemptively in the course of events, working toward wholeness in relationships, the appropriate direction of expectation for human beings is toward full participation in unfolding life. There are religions which encourage escape through shrinking back, regression, denial or distortion of facts, or transference to another world. There are religions which encourage movement toward wholeness and fulfillment. The Christian experience of hope discerns God at work *within* history, *within* the events and conditions and processes which profoundly condition our being. Thus, the Christian experience of God and of hope encourages the freedom to move more deeply into life, to participate in the risks and responsibilities and rewards of mature involvement.

The love of God includes both discipline and permissiveness: the discipline implicit in the basic structures and conditions of reality, the permissiveness implicit in life's "letting-be" in the uniqueness of one's being. God judges man but does not condemn him for his finitude. There are threatening aspects in the world with which man must deal, but there is also a dimension of caring written into the deepest nature of reality. The love of God is *the ultimate caring*. The love of God gives life to man, accepts man as having a right to be, provides conditions for growth toward wholeness, makes possible the growth of meaning within the inescapable limitations to which individuals are subject, introduces potentiality in all that man experiences, provides resources for enduring, recovery, for renewal and new beginnings. The love of God is manifest in the profundity of vicarious suffering through which healing and new life are mediated. The love of God links life with life in bonds of fellow-feeling, shared work and play, and love and creativity. The love of God permits and encourages man to grow toward and into maturity, coming to participate in God's whole-making work not as a dependent child, but as an adult working on a side-by-side basis with other human beings and working with God. The parent-child analogy carried through in reference to the God-man relationship says that the love of God permits the child to grow into adulthood and to have an adult relationship with the God whose work is unending.

The love of God is manifest in that gracious working whereby man is permitted to become an instrument of whole-making in the world, an agent of creation and reconciliation in the midst of the pain and wonder of existence. The love of God binds man to man in bonds through which the influence of one part is multiplied many times in the larger life of the whole. The love of God is manifest in that provision whereby the lifework of one person is gathered into the larger pattern of reality and so, in ways past our fully knowing, contributes to the enduring reality of God.

In the light of this vision of God's love toward man, the meaning of man's love toward God becomes more clear. To love God is to accept the gift of life with reverent hands and to seek the realization of one's finest potentialities within the limits life imposes. It is to say "yes" to life and to the whole pattern of life, including death. It is to be open to life's healing and renewing resources and to seek the potential, values, and meanings in each day and situation. It is to give oneself to the passing circumstance so fully that the moment is brought to fullness and its glory revealed. It is to seek more creative linkages with all that has being, organic and inorganic. It is to affirm in his uniqueness and potentials the selfhood of the other person with whom one deals. It is to exercise the grace of giving and receiving. It is to participate in God's "letting-be" in relationships with other persons, including those over whom one exercises power. It is to respect the potential wholeness of the other and ardently to desire his growth.

Love toward God involves openness to what the day or hour or situation may bring forth, an attentiveness to the call for understanding and caring and loving that comes out of the heart of life. Love toward God issues in the noblest form of prayer, the unceasing prayer of life reaching beyond itself for expression and fulfillment in relation to the divine source and goal of life. To love God is to worship God in the affirmation of life with one's whole being—heart, soul, strength, and mind. To love God is to give oneself to the unending quest for oneness with God through oneness with his creatures. To love God is to live in joy, tension, and in aspiration between what is and what might be.

Christian faith, in its mature expressions, is open to the living witness of all men of goodwill everywhere. It affirms that the living Word becomes flesh and dwells in the midst of men whenever and wherever the love of God is mediated through persons bringing wholeness of life and hope. God is in Christ reconciling the world to himself wherever the love of God is declared in word and deed and relationship in the midst of joy and fulfillment; of pain, conflict, injustice, sorrow, ignorance, and need. God is revealed in present as well as in past events. Christ, the revealing person, comes again and again. The witnessing-serving-reconciling community of faith is reborn wherever there are those who unite in commitment to the living Christ and who in the spirit of the God of love declare and mediate his word of grace and wholeness. Just as the God-question is asked by the whole person, so the entire person affirms the reality of God in his trusting, hoping, growing, serving, and loving.

LIVING IN THE LIGHT OF GOD'S REALITY

Part Three

17. Celebrating the Gift of Our Own Uniqueness

TO AFFIRM and celebrate life in its wholeness, each of us needs to recognize himself as a person of worth and to be known as a person of worth. How we understand ourselves and feel about ourselves is of crucial importance. Our perception of how other people think and feel about us is of almost equal importance. Harry Stack Sullivan said that the self is "made up of reflected appraisals." The struggle to find a sense of identity and personal worth is one of the central concerns of human living.

Making Friends With Oneself

Dwight Moody once observed that he had had more difficulty with himself than with any other person he had ever met. Most of us could say the same. To accept oneself, to say "yes" to life's invitation to enact the human role *as oneself*, to celebrate the gift of one's own uniqueness, is no easy matter. Yet, to fail in this is to miss fulfillment. The only condition on which life is offered an individual is on the basis of *being himself*.

Coming to a sense of personal worth is sometimes difficult because a person feels "I am different from other persons." A thoughtful person is aware of his handicaps and the limitations under which he must live. No one else can possibly occupy precisely the same space one occupies physically, mentally, or emotionally. Some sense of isolation is inherent in being an individual. In this sense of isolation and "being different," one's self-esteem is threatened.

One's own baffling nature complicates the movement toward fulfillment. Each of us experiences inner conflicts of feelings, desires, values, and purposes. Each of us experiences inner tensions in decision-making. Each of us experiences the inner turmoil of seeming to be both child and adult, loving and hating, self-centered and altruistic at the same time. It is difficult to accept ourselves because we do not know who or what we are! Sometimes we feel like the character in a novel who was described as being "not so much a human being as a civil war."

Accepting oneself and growing toward a mature sense of personal worth is further complicated by various subtle forms of self-rejection. Sometimes one inwardly rejects himself because he feels he is rejected by other persons and by life itself. Sometimes one rejects himself because of failures he has experienced or mistakes he has made. Sometimes, strangely enough, one condemns himself for being a finite creature. Unfortunately, some religion actually nurtures feelings of guilt in persons because of limitations inherent in finitude. In the failure to reach goals or standards which no finite person could possibly reach, some persons condemn themselves.

In the Bible we find the injunction to "Love your neighbor as yourself." We have mounting evidence indicating that it is humanly impossible to love other persons in a mature way, or to love being alive as a person, so long as one is basically rejecting himself. Thus, a crucial struggle goes on in the depths of each person's inner life. This struggle has to do with one's own self-evaluation, self-perception, and self-acceptance or self-rejection.

One of the major contributions of mature religion is in helping persons come to a realistic assessment of self and of the human situation. Mature religion nurtures a wholesome self-respect in relation to the whole of being, provides resources for dealing with blockages to self-acceptance, and invites each person to celebrate the gift of his own uniqueness.

Seeing Oneself in Perspective

Fundamental to the theological point of view of this book is the conviction that self-understanding requires sensitivity to the supreme context in which all human beings rightly belong. With the gift of life come possibilities and demands. To understand the larger framework of our being is better to understand what is entailed in a truly human existence. Knowledge of God involves knowledge of what is given us and what is demanded of us if we are to take our place in the divine pattern of reality.

To see life in its ultimate context is to discern the basic human role more clearly. We all enact a number of roles in relation to nature, work, family, church, special groups, community, nation, world. But fundamental to these varied roles is the supreme role defined by the character of the wholeness of which we are a part, *the role of being human and growing in humanness.* Reality in its wholeness provides for many creatures, with different roles. To see reality in its wholeness is to see man's relatedness to other beings. It is also to recognize such distinctively human capacities as thinking, reflection, self-transcendence, the making of moral distinctions, creativity, decision-making, worship.

To see oneself in the perspective of wholeness is to recognize oneself as having a unique status in a vast, awesome drama of cosmic dimensions. It is to see oneself as a biological, psychological, and sociological creature. It is also to see oneself as a creature called to participate in deciding directions to be taken in the evolutionary processes. To recognize in the call to growing humanness the call of God as ultimate meaningfulness is to recognize a dimension of enduring worth in one's own existence. It is also to recognize that one is endowed with the power and responsibility to make the crucial decision for or against enacting the basic human role. As human creatures we are both bound and free. In the interrelatedness of limitation and possibility there is an area wherein we may exercise a "margin for initiative." We ourselves have something to say about whether we shall play the role of clod or cog or little god —or that of a human being moving toward the realization of possibilities. In the decision for or against self-affirmation, we prove something of the wonder of human nature in relation to the whole of being. Each of us celebrates the gift of his own uniqueness.

Human Nature Being What It Is—and Isn't

The vision of reality in its wholeness illuminates the possibilities which inhere in human nature. Distorted views of human nature sometimes grow out of piecemeal or fragmented perceptions of human functioning. To see a whole person in the context of wholeness is to recognize in man the amazing interplay of maturity and immaturity, self-centeredness and altruism, good and evil, fear and courage, love and hate, honesty and deception, destructiveness and creativity, shrinking back and moving forward.

A holistic approach helps to make sense out of the seemingly paradoxical behavior of man. It sees man functioning in diversified and changing settings with varied motivations. Man seeks a life-style in which he can function with relative security and satisfaction. In groping and struggling to find this life-style, he engages in both constructive and destructive behaviors. The deeply human desires for security, adventure, recognition, response, expression, and fulfillment are involved in the noblest and most creative purposes and activities of man. They are also involved in the most cruel and destructive things man does. To see man in his total functioning is to see him as a dynamic and relational creature often blocked and frustrated along the way, coping with situations sometimes constructively, sometimes destructively. Such an approach points to the view that man is neither inherently good nor inherently evil. He is a creature of amazing potentiality given to trying out many ways of moving toward his goals in quest for fulfillment.

The holistic approach to an understanding of man reveals him as endowed with the capacity for growing toward maturity in humanness through frustration and struggle, joy and achievement. In this capacity is the agony and glory of mankind, and hope for and in the human situation. To what extent this hope is realized will depend on the ways in which human beings are reared, the values they internalize, the social inventions they appropriate, the goals after which they strive, the visions by which they come to live, the decisions they make. To commit oneself to the whole-making purposes of God in the time and place in which one lives is to move toward human fulfillment.

Thus, no human being stands condemned for his human nature. On the contrary, by virtue of the reality of God he is accepted and invited to participate in the adventure of self-discovery, the making of new beginnings and growth. He is invited each day to savor life in its manifold richness. He is invited to be receptive to the gracious working whereby fragments of life may be woven into patterns of new meaning, to grow toward a healthy conscience in commitment to self-chosen goals, to internalize values long growing in family, community, government, science, art, philosophy, and religion. He is invited to relate himself to causes of significance, to participate in the processes of whole-making, to give himself to the world in his uniqueness.

To be a person is to be a center of feeling, thinking, hurting, valuing, aspiring. Though each of us has much in common with other persons, no one in all history has experienced *my* thoughts and feelings precisely as *I* experience them. No one else has ever suffered *my* particular combination of limitations and possibilities. To accept life on the terms it is offered and to give oneself to the living of each day with integrity, is to worship God in celebrating the gift of one's own uniqueness.

Coming to a Basic Image of Self and Life

C. Wright Mills, the sociologist, spoke of "the great salesroom" image of human relations and of life. In terms of this image, life is for consuming and selling and getting. Success is measured in the values of the marketplace. Whatever sense of personal worth or self-acceptance one achieves in the light of this image is within the framework of these values.

To see life in the vision of wholeness, and to commit oneself to the God ever seeking greater wholeness of being, is to live with quite another image. The significant life is not so much the consuming-selling life as the creating-sharing-whole-making life.

The purposiveness in living, in this image, is in self-discovery, self-actualization, self-investment in the significant. It is in the caring which receives from others and gives to others. It is in giving the other person his self-respect, even as I permit him to give me mine. The purposiveness of life in the image of wholeness is the enactment of varied roles in family, community, work, recreation, and so on, but all within the framework of the basic human role of living courageously, sensitively, creatively, lovingly in relation to reality in its wholeness.

To see one's own life and that of other human beings in this light is to discern sanctity in existence and in the human enterprise. It is to know the worth of being alive as a person. It is to discover a firm basis for self-acceptance and self-affirmation. To accept the gift of life in this light is to celebrate the gift of one's own uniqueness as a human being. It is to worship the God of life.

18.

Celebrating Human Dignity in the Midst of Adversity

INTO THE LIFE of every human being comes the experience of adversity. Disappointment, suffering, and death are a part of the life of man. Under these circumstances how can we speak of the celebration of life in its wholeness? How can we speak of the reality and love of God in the presence of agony, injustice, and death?

Intellectual integrity forbids that we close our eyes to the facts of loss and tragedy. The statements "All is for the best" or "God wills it so" or "Someday we shall understand" fail to satisfy many persons who seek a positive faith by which to deal with the realities of daily experience. Such persons want to see things as they really are and to affirm such faith as they can without compromising their intellectual integrity.

Three questions pertaining to a theological interpretation of adversity press in upon us: (1) How can we account for the fact of adversity in a world which is said to be good and purposeful? (2) What is the relation of God to human experiences of adversity? (3) How can man deal with adversity, maintaining his sense of the goodness and purposefulness of existence?

Adversity and the Vision of Wholeness

Matthew Arnold paid tribute to the friend "who saw life steadily, and saw it whole." To face the adversities of life in steadiness of spirit does, indeed, involve some vision of reality in its wholeness. Seen by itself, a given event may appear to be all evil; seen in a context of events, it may be perceived differently. Seeing reality in relation to patterns of wholeness does not eliminate the fact of evil, but specific evils sometimes come to have changed meanings. To say "taking all things into account" or "in the long run" or "everything considered" is to introduce a new and important dimension into any discussion. Nothing said or written can remove the stark fact of misfortune, suffering, and tragedy nor answer all the questions they raise. Yet, out of our deepest insights into reality in its wholeness, and out of the examples of persons who demonstrate that even adversity sometimes provides a soil for meaning, there are some affirmations which can and should be made.

One relevant consideration is that there are risks involved in the experience of being human. Human life involves a measure of sensitivity, of freedom, the capacity to make some decisions, human interrelatedness in bonds of meaning and responsibility, the capacity for growth. In the long run we would wish it to be so. We recognize that many of the deepest meanings and highest values of life flow from these conditions. Yet these same conditions are often implicated in the most devastating experiences. A great deal of human distress can be traced to misjudgment and the misuse of freedom, to events and experiences related to our close human relationships, to our reluctance to leave long-cherished beliefs or judgments or ways of doing things in order to grow into fuller maturity. Human finitude involves strengths and limitations both of which may issue in fulfillment or adversity. Apparently satisfaction and suffering are often cut from the same cloth. When specific adversities come our way we may first react by counting them all evil. Seen in the perspective of the whole life of man, some misfortune is recognized as being inevitable. To be fully human is continually to be subject to adversity. Only the insensitive creature is spared that destiny.

The risk of adversity inheres not only in the nature of man but in the nature of reality in its wider reaches. A pluralistic universe is not designed for the absolute security and guaranteed well-being of any one creature. It is a universe of "many ends." Furthermore, a dynamic, interrelated, and evolutionary universe, including myriads of realities with a measure of self-determination (from atoms to human beings) involves not only the possibility but the near-inevitability of collisions and chance happenings. Some of the good and evil in the world is a matter of timing. How events come to be related to each other may issue in good or evil, joy or sorrow, frustration or fulfillment. A static or completely determined universe might conceivably be a universe without certain kinds of adversity. A dynamic, interrelated, evolutionary universe involving sensitive growing creatures with a measure of self-determination is potential for good and evil, adversity and satisfaction. To recognize that much adversity is not planned and that the possibility of misfortune inheres in reality in its wholeness does not make specific adversities less real. However, it may enable one to see life more steadily in times of testing. It may also alleviate the pain of self-blame in some situations, and in others the feeling of being the object of cruel purpose.

As a creature born for growth in sensitive and creative humanness in a dynamic and pluralistic universe, man is in a situation both hazardous and wonderful. Specific adversities usually come as a surprise. Yet, the ever-present possibility of adversity is a fact to be recognized.

To affirm goodness and purposefulness in creation is not to deny the reality or the inevitability of tragedy, suffering, and death. It is to affirm the possibility of meaningful existence in a world in which these ravaging facts are personally experienced. Indeed, some forms of meaning are experienced, not despite the most devastating events of life, but through them. The same basic conditions and processes which sometimes issue in adversity are also implicated in the coming of the highest values and greatest joys we experience. There is a dimension of wholeness in reality which illuminates the working out of specific events.

Discerning God in the Midst of Adversity

Once we give up the concept of a God who plans or imposes specific instances of suffering the questions emerge, "How can we speak meaningfully of the reality of God in the presence of life's most difficult experiences? In what sense, if any, can the love and purposefulness of God be affirmed in the presence of human anguish and death? What is the relation of God to the tragic suffering involved in war, incurable disease, hunger, ignorance, life-impairing accidents, and torn human relationships?"

In previous chapters God has been referred to as the Wholeness-Reality. As such, God is understood to be the ground of wholeness, the character of reality making for wholeness. Again, it has been affirmed that God is the ordering, uniting, creating, value-conserving reality conjoining the integrity of the individual with the integrity of other individuals with the integrity of the whole. The word "God" points to the dimension of wholeness in reality. God makes the difference between cosmos and chaos.

To think of God in these terms is to relinquish the idea of God as a being standing completely outside the course of events in which man lives and moves and has his being. On the contrary, it is to affirm the reality of God as profoundly involved in the course of events in ordering, creating, conserving, but often in noncoercive ways. God is the fundamental character of reality by virtue of which men are made bold to affirm the adventure of life even under the most adverse circumstances. God is the fundamental integrity of reality by virtue of which men are all subject to a "kind impartiality" in the working out of events, by virtue of which there is a connection between deeds and consequences, and by virtue of which exploitive, destructive actions are self-defeating in the long run. Einstein referred to "the rationality made manifest in existence." The word "God" refers to that character of reality in the light of which reality may be investigated by rational minds; but God is more. God is the Wholeness-Reality sustaining and undergirding the life of integrity. In the midst of adversity God is present, not as a being who protects individuals from all difficulty, but as the ultimate reality by virtue of which adversity may be seen within a pattern of order and potentiality.

When a young person of great promise, in whom much has been invested, is stricken with an incurable disease, one may well question the goodness of reality. Obviously such a tragedy is *not* good. No explanation can remove the tragic dimension of such an event. Nevertheless, the physical aspects of such an occurrence are understandable within the framework of an orderly, dynamic, evolutionary universe. The processes by which men live and die, fall ill and are healed can be investigated by rational minds. Through investigation and experimentation these processes yield their secrets. A single tragedy is not the measure of all reality. It gives its vivid testimony to the tragic dimension of reality. But it also points to the larger context of events in which order prevails over chaos. If this were not the case, life could not continue to go on.

God is also present in the midst of adversity as undergirding strength and sustaining presence. Some of the most significant literature ever written has been by persons who have discovered that in the solitude of disappointment, suffering, and loss they were not alone. Robert Pfeiffer, distinguished Old Testament scholar, wrote that the inwardness of Jewish piety reached its noblest expression in the words of the seventy-third Psalm, "My flesh and my heart may fail, but God is the strength of my heart and my portion for ever" (PSALMS 73:26). Through the centuries persons have varied, partly because of differences in temperament, in their sense of the reality of God's sustaining presence. But multitudes have affirmed and do affirm that in adversity they have experienced the companionship of the Divine-Real-Other, bringing a dimension of depth and meaning to what externally seems evil. A wise man of old said, "Count no experience all evil if through it you are brought closer to God, for God is the greatest good."

God is present in adversity as that reality in the light of which experiences which have been counted wasted, evil, or tragic may be gathered into some new pattern of meaning, purpose, and wholeness. The reality of God is mediated by persons who reveal that adversity can be redemptive.

Mark Rutherford spoke of "that silent promptitude of nature which rebels not at a wound but the very next instant begins her work of protection and recovery."[1] In the wondrous processes of healing, we discern a more-than-human reality working for and toward wholeness. The same healing reality manifest in relation to a physical wound is present in the redemptive processes through which an experience once counted all loss becomes a factor in a new pattern of meaning. Through adversity a growth and deepening of the spirit sometimes takes place, bonds of sympathy and insight are deepened, sensitivity to life's qualitative dimension is kindled, an openness to new perspectives and to new chapters of experience comes into being. It has been said that pain conquered is power. The experience of pain may issue in inner defeat; it may also issue in a more inward life and in a life which brings strength, insight, courage, and healing to others.

The reality of God does not guarantee that all adversity will be redemptive in the sense of issuing in some good. But the reality of God makes redemptive adversity a possibility. God is the reality working in and through all forms of experience toward patterns of integrity and wholeness. The purposiveness of God is that the potential meaningfulness of events should be realized. The love of God is manifest in the provision that man has a voice in determining what events will do and mean to him. The love of God is the divine caring which respects the integrity of the individual under all conditions and works with him in using adversity in the creation of a significant life.

Declaring Oneself in the Presence of Adversity

In his book *Man's Search for Meaning*, Dr. Viktor Frankl reports the reactions of persons to the indignities endured in Nazi prison camps. He wrote:

> What was really needed was a fundamental change in our attitude toward life. We had to learn ourselves and, furthermore, we had to teach the despairing men, that it did not really matter what we expected from life, but rather what life expected from us. We needed to stop asking about the meaning of life, and instead to think of ourselves as those who were being questioned by life —daily and hourly. Our answer must consist, not in talk and meditation, but in right action and in right conduct. Life ultimately means taking the responsibility to find the right answer to its problems and to fulfill the tasks which it constantly sets for each individual.[2]

In this and other passages, Dr. Frankl stresses the importance of the individual's own *decision for meaning* in the midst of adversity. We are not able to control all external circumstances, but we do have a voice in determining what those circumstances will mean to us. Thus, *the experience of suffering provides a unique opportunity for celebrating one's own selfhood and dignity in the midst of adversity.*

Persons do not always choose what role they will play in life, but they do have a voice in determining how well the role will be played. Reality in its wholeness has a place for persons who serve the world in the role of mature sufferers. In the working out of events, some persons are cast in a disadvantaged role they would not have chosen. Just as work may be seen as a vocation (calling), so inescapable adversity may call forth the sense of vocation. Adversity may be the vehicle by which some persons declare the greatness of the human spirit. Some of the noblest and most useful lives ever lived have been lived by persons who have given living proof that the human self is greater than external limitations and misfortunes.

What life comes to mean to any human being depends in no small measure on the outcome of his personal encounters with disappointment, suffering, and loss. Such encounters are never easy, and sometimes they are devastating. But whether adversity in a final sense is something that happens *to* us or *in* us makes the crucial difference, and each person has something to say about which it will be. Seeing adversity in relation to reality in its wholeness, discerning God in the midst of adversity, and recognizing that in the midst of adversity one may declare himself as a person of worth and strength of spirit, tips the scales between hoping and despairing.

19.

The Celebration of Life in Devotion and Prayer

MUCH THEOLOGICAL writing in recent years has emphasized the ethical-social-political dimensions of religion while saying relatively little about the inner life of devotion and prayer. God, we are being told, is where the action is.

Nevertheless, many persons are recognizing that one cannot have the fruits of religion without the roots, and the roots reach deep into man's inner life in relation to God. It is a hopeful sign that the question is being asked, "How are the inner and outer dimensions of the life of faith related?"

If God is the Wholeness-Reality, as we have been affirming, it is appropriate to speak of the presense of God in relation to the inner life of devotion as well as to the life of ethical decision, social service, and social action. If the religious life involves commitment on all levels of experience in response to the vision of God, we may reasonably anticipate cognitive, esthetic, affective, and moral expressions of the life of faith. In this chapter we shall consider the experiences of mysticism and prayer in the light of the perception of God as the Wholeness-Reality.

The Mystical Dimension of Religious Experience

In every age there are persons who report deep feelings of kinship, rapport, union with the divine, or with what they believe to be central and enduring in reality. Such persons testify to the awareness of the presence of the ultimately real. Rufus Jones, the Quaker mystic, defined mysticism as "an immediate, intuitive, experimental knowledge of God, or one may say it is consciousness of a Beyond, or of a transcendent Reality, or of Divine Presence."[1] Mystics report varying degrees of intensity in their experiences, all the way from a sense of not being alone even in solitude, to intense and unforgettable experiences of divine confrontation and presence. Most testimonies to the mystic form of religious experience indicate that it is deeply rewarding, reassuring, and satisfying, but also unamenable to verbal description or articulation. He who has sensed the presence of God is likely to regard this experience as self-authenticating; no rational argument is needed to justify or explain it. Many persons regard the mystic experience as being the supreme expression of religion.

Some mystics claim that a distinctive kind of knowledge comes through the mystic experience. The mystic, they affirm, is privileged to see directly into the inner nature of reality in its wholeness. He finds it good and trustworthy. Mysticism as a philosophy asserts that reality is One, that it is indescribable, that it is identical with the essence of the human self, and that union with the One is possible. Some mystics assert that reason and scientific investigation at best can tell us something about parts or fragments of reality; it is only in the mystic experience that reality in its wholeness is experienced and known.

Mystics differ on the question of whether preparations can be made for the mystical experience. Some apparently believe that it comes and goes independently of human effort. Other mystics have said that preparation in purgation, illumination, and contemplation may help. François Fenelon wrote, "The wind of God is always blowing, but you must hoist your sail."

Although religious mystics affirm that their experience convinces them of the reality of God, others take a more tentative approach. James Bissett Pratt cited the case of a man who spoke of something akin to mystical experience while insisting that theologically speaking he was an agnostic:

> I seem to feel within the depths of my being an action, a presence; in short I seem to be the object, even prior to being the subject, of an action that is spiritual. . . . I tell myself that this sensation may itself be an illusion, that there may be nothing real about it apart from my subjectivity; but it *is*, and that is enough for me to live by. . . . It is a part of my being and has for the rest of my being an importance and a value that are supreme—that suffices me.[2]

Statements such as that just quoted remind us that the experience of "presence" is not confined to persons who affirm the reality of God in a more or less traditional sense. There is an experience of presence, of relatedness of spirit to reality in its wholeness, which may or may not be given a theological interpretation. Although persons vary greatly in temperament, it is probably true that there is something of the mystic in most persons. There are times when one feels the reality and the presence of what William James called "the More" which in some sense acts on man and is responsive to him.

What is to be said of the mystical experience in the light of a theology which understands God to be the Wholeness-Reality? Three comments are in order.

First, if reality is best understood in dynamic-relational terms, the interplay of parts and wholes, and if man is a creation of reality in its wholeness, it would be reasonable to assume that something like the mystical experience would be known to man. In this light, the feeling of kinship or oneness with reality in its depths and wholeness ought not be regarded as strange or abnormal or illusory. On the contrary, insofar as man is open and receptive to reality in its fullness and qualitative dimensions it may be anticipated that he will sometimes be grasped in the depths of his being by the Real-Other to which he is ultimately related.

Second, if the reality of man is in his wholeness (body, mind, spirit), then the mystical dimension of life is not to be regarded as an isolated experience, but as bearing upon man's experience in its totality. Theologies which stress a sharp distinction between body and mind, flesh and spirit, sometimes encourage a world-withdrawal form of mysticism. The mystic is regarded as one who draws closer to God by withdrawing from the normal events and experiences of life.

When God is understood to be the Wholeness-Reality, the mystic experience is understood in another way. The sense of the presence of God is understood in relation to the varied rhythms of life involving thought, feeling, action. To be sure, the individual may withdraw for a time from the pressing immediacies and demands of life for worship, mediation, and communion, but he withdraws in order that he might reenter the world with clearer vision and renewal of spirit.

In his classic work *The Meaning of God in Human Experience,* William Ernest Hocking discussed the "principle of alternation." It was Hocking's thesis that the fullest and most adequate life-style involves alternation in attention to part and whole, world and God, self and not-self, activity and passivity, work and worship. It is in this alternation that reality is experienced most fully. God as Wholeness-Reality evokes the will both to work and to worship, to commune and to create. The whole person does not always have a vivid feeling of the presence of God; he knows the "tides of the spirit." But insofar as he does experience the feeling of God's real presence, his inner life is renewed, his basic confidence in the worthfulness of existence is undergirded, and he moves into the world of work and responsibility from a center of trust and commitment. Dr. Hocking wrote:

> Any given moment of life must choose between two goods, psychologically incompatible. On the one hand, the peace of the hermit, the silence of the forest, the exaltation of sacrifice, the mightiness of simplification and unity, the joy of self-abandonment, the calm of absolute contemplation, the vision of God. On the other hand, the variety and stress of life, the zest of common ends, the mastery of means, the glory of infinite enterprise, the pride of creativity and self-possession. The modern world has made its choice. But there is a better choice: namely, the choice of both. For the life of each is that it may lose itself, from time to time, in the life of the other. And this, which is obvious in things partial, is true—and even chiefly true—in things total.[3]

Third, if God is the Wholeness-Reality, it is appropriate that man should consciously seek to be open to those promptings of the spirit and visitations of divine presence to which the mystics witness. Our preoccupation with immediacies and parts of reality needs to be balanced with times of attention to the larger and more inclusive reality of which we are a part. In times of reflection, contemplation, and communion, there may come the inner persuasion that in the midst of life we are dealing with a responsive and trustworthy Real-Other. If man is indeed linked with a reality which is more than the sum total of the fragmentary pieces of his existence, it is the part of wisdom to make a place for those disciplines of mind and spirit which direct man's aspirations toward the Ultimate.

In his autobiography Charles Darwin reported that as a

young man he found great pleasure in poetry, drama, and music, but that as the years passed he neglected these resources in his preoccupation with other matters. Something of importance went out of his life in the process. He said that if he had his life to live over he would make it a rule to read some poetry and listen to music every week, and so live a richer, more satisfying life. In similar fashion, the mystic reminds us of a dimension of life which enlarges the world of human experience and enriches each moment with an awareness of that Reality which gathers up and transcends all individual moments.

Prayer in the Life of Wholeness

Prayer in some form is practiced by countless persons throughout the world. In varied ways men directly address the deity in which or in whom they believe, employing appropriate words, attitudes, and postures.

Men pray under varied circumstances: in stress and danger, in joy, in bewilderment, in times of inner struggle, in moments of communion, in rather ordinary situations as thoughts are turned Godward. There are prayers of praise, petition, meditation, and mystical communion. There is variation in the words, attitudes, and postures which men use and assume in prayer, but always they are designed to express what is in the mind and heart and purpose of man as he addresses his deity. Men bring differing expectations to the experience of prayer, but the universal intention of prayer is to relate the individual or praying group to the divine.

Prayer is practiced among persons who differ in their concepts of God. It is sometimes assumed that prayer is possible and appropriate only when God is believed to be a supernatural being who attends personally to the prayers of each individual. However, in Jainism and in some Buddhism, prayer is practiced even though no direct response is anticipated from the religious object. The theory is that through prayer man may relate himself to the ultimate reality without necessary thought of reciprocity. Again, in some religious thought God is perceived to be an all-encompassing spiritual reality with which the individual may relate in prayer, sometimes losing personal identity in the ocean of the divine reality. Thus, the impulse to pray is expressed in widely differing situations and in relation to widely differing concepts of God.

A relationship exists between an individual's personal religious experience and his concept of God. On the one hand, his personal experience influences the way he thinks about God. On the other hand, his concept of God influences and gives direction to his religious life. Thus, one's perception of the divine reality inevitably has a bearing on one's thoughts and feelings about prayer. Whether or not one prays is not determined exclusively by what he thinks about God, but his beliefs are extremely important in this matter. Many persons have either stopped praying or started praying with changes in their views of God.

To believe in God as the Wholeness-Reality is to discourage certain approaches to prayer and to encourage others. In a theology which discerns God as Ultimate Reality in an order which is dynamic, relational, and evolutionary in character, there is no place for magical views of prayer, using God to achieve the ends of the one who prays. Neither is there place for prayers designed to circumvent or interrupt the fundamental structures and processes of reality. It is inappropriate and irreverent to use prayer to deny the character of God! On the other hand, new and richer possibilities in prayer begin to emerge once we move beyond magical approaches to the God-man relationship.

In speaking of the life of devotion, it is important to recognize that there are differences among persons in the ways they relate to the world of nature, to other persons, and to reality in its wholeness. Prayer is one of many ways of relating to God. It is unrealistic to assume that all persons of religious belief and commitment will find equal meanings in prayer. Something of the mystical temperament appears to be a prerequisite of a sustained life of prayer, and individuals vary in this respect. Nevertheless, many individuals who long assumed that prayer had no meaning for them have been surprised to discover that prayer opened the door to wider and richer dimensions of experience than they had thought possible. Through prayer they have become alive in a new way.

A distinction needs to be drawn between the *intent* and the *content* of specific prayers. Prayer is a human attempt to bring one's life into the light and presence of God and to respond to the reality of God. The languages used in prayer are often inadequate, but more important than the specific content of prayer is its intent. To acknowledge and attend to the reality of God is the important aspect of prayer. It is a turning from preoccupation with self to God experienced as source and grace and goal. We pray, not because we have come to final knowledge of God, but because we aspire after a deeper and fuller relationship with God. The language of prayer expresses this aspiration.

Prayer in relationship to the Wholeness-Reality probably has elements of autosuggestion in it, but it is more. There is a divine dimension to autosuggestion in its most creative forms. However, God as Wholeness-Reality is more than the sum of all human parts; God transcends all particular persons, events, and times even while immanent in them and foundational to them. To leave God out of man's accounting is to neglect the ultimate reality from which life comes and in which life is fulfilled. Prayer is the most direct and articulate means man has at his disposal for acknowledging the reality of God and for seeking to relate his life to God in trust and devotion. To *say* something is to put oneself into a situation and to make it one's own in a distinctive way. In prayer the God-man relationship is internalized, the God of theory becomes *my* God. While prayer may not be absolutely essential to a meaningful life of faith, in practice the man of faith is normally a man who prays. Prayer undergirds, nurtures, and deepens his faith.

In a theology which perceives God as the Wholeness-Reality, prayer is not an exercise added to the various activities of life. Rather, *prayer is experience coming to expression in relation to the source and goal of life*. Thus, the most meaningful prayer rises out of situations in which we most deeply feel the danger, joy, struggle, and possibilities of our own inner and relational existence. To approach God in reverence, trust, and hope in the midst of fear, uncertainty, tragedy, struggle, intellectual searching, remorse, joy, fulfillment, weakness, and strength is to pray. Words and postures will usually be involved in the praying, but these are of secondary importance to the intent of the praying. Of all the answers to prayer, the greatest is God's gift of his own presence. To pray is to know that one is not ultimately alone. To pray is to acknowledge that one has not reached the point of final despair. To pray is to hope. To pray is to affirm life in its wholeness.

20.
A Morality of Celebration

MAN IS A deciding creature. Unlike a clod or cog, man places the stamp of his own thinking, feeling, valuing, and deciding upon the course of events. Therein lies both the pain and wonder of being human.

Man is both bound and free. Some factors in his experience are beyond his control; to be human is to live within limitations. On the other hand, in many situations man is confronted by alternatives. He is free to choose among various possible attitudes, goals, ways of acting. Even in adverse circumstances man has some word to say as to how he will react to what is beyond his external control. The capacity for decision-making is a distinguishing mark of the human creature.

Demands for decision are confronted in various types of situations and relationships. Some are deeply personal and relate primarily to oneself. Others have to do with person-to-person relationships in which two individuals are primarily involved. Some decision-making situations emerge within intimate groups, such as the family. Others have to do with one's work. Still others relate to one's life as a citizen where community or national policies, practices, and procedures are at stake. The decisions we make involve such diverse matters as the spending of time, money, or energy, how we vote, how we relate to other human beings, how we act in business, family, or community, and so on. How one responds to decision-making situations is crucial in determining what sort of person he becomes. Even the endeavor to avoid responsibility in decision-making becomes a kind of decision with attendant consequences.

Morality has to do with attitudes, values, goals, policies, and courses of action for which persons decide in actual situations. Morality or lack of it is disclosed, not in general theories about right or wrong which are affirmed, but in actual decisions which are made. Morality has reference to situations in which persons declare themselves, their values, their purposes, their essential life style in the context of specific sets of events through decisions which are made.

A distinction needs to be drawn between morality in the sense of *acting out* and ethics in the sense of *reflecting upon* the bases of morality. Insofar as man is a rational creature, he is capable of reflecting upon himself, his situation, and his varied responses to his life-situation. He is able critically to evaluate alternative courses of action in terms of appropriateness and possible consequences. Insofar as man is free, he is able to choose between alternative courses of action. Insofar as man is a whole creature, he is able to relate his rational, affective, and volitional capacities in the context of specific situations. The whole person has an ethical concern, but the ultimate relevance of his ethical concern is found in his functioning as a human being in situations which are potential for good and evil, for life-enhancement and life-impoverishment. The acid test of the morality of a person or group is not in what is theoretically held to be good or desirable, but in the means and ends, the concern for consequences, and the openness to the future which are revealed in the making of actual decisions.

Nevertheless, mature morality presupposes the background of serious thought and reflection which is the concern of ethics.

What does it mean to see a decision-making situation in a perspective of wholeness? What is the relevance of God as the Wholeness-Reality to decision-making? What are the implications for decision-making in an image of man as a creature who is fulfilled in a life of wholeness and whole-making? These questions relate the ethical and moral concerns as man seeks both a theory of appropriate human behavior and greater competence in responsible decision-making.

Seeing Decision Situations in Context

To bring the perspective of wholeness to bear on a decision-making situation is to endeavor to see that situation in its varied contexts. It is to take into account past, present, and future. It is to take into account the constituent factors and events of the situation. It is to take into account the forces which are shaping events. It is to take into account the social and cosmic contexts. It is to bring to bear upon the choices and decisions one makes the most inclusive possible philosophy of life. Obviously, no one fully reaches this ideal in decision-making, but the holistic approach to moral issues seeks the most comprehensive possible perspective.

In the light of reality in its wholeness *the principle of respect for the integrity of self and the other* takes on major significance. Man is part of a whole from which he cannot resign. The integrity of the whole presupposes integrity of parts and integrity in the relationships of parts and wholes. The highest morality is that which celebrates the dignity and integrity of man in his relationships with all that partakes in being. The highest morality is a celebration of life in its wholeness. Man is that creature who is called to be human and to grow in humanness. There is a cosmic claim upon him to fulfill the human role. The morality of wholeness is a celebrating response to that claim. It is a morality which affirms life, which seeks the enhancement of life, which savors life, which respects both the limitations and possibilities of life, which seeks the increasing welfare of all human life as mankind moves into new chapters of history. In the larger patterns of reality man is called to be man. Morality is man's witness and serious response to that call in the decision-making situations of life.

The vision of wholeness reveals reality to be dynamic, pluralistic, interrelated, evolutionary, and marked by the interplay of parts and wholes. The implications of this vision of reality for morality are far-reaching. One of the most important implications is that *mature morality is an art rather than a legalistic application of fixed rules.* As broad a generalization as we can make in the light of an holistic approach to moral issues is the principle of respect for the integrity of self and of the other to whom one is related. To bring the vision of integrity to bear upon specific situations requires the intelligence, sensitivity, imagination, and creativity of the true artist. Artistry in morality involves respect for the uniqueness of each moment, each situation, each relationship. It involves a recognition that different situations are potential for different values and meanings. Artistry in morality involves decision-making in the light of sensitivity to the potentiality of persons and situations.

Artistry in morality likewise involves the sympathy and imagination required to enter into the perspective of other persons, to see and to feel with them in the context of specific situations. It involves the attempt to make impartial judgments in the light of relevant facts. It involves a recognition that each situation presents both limitations and possibilities. Mature morality aims at the realization of integrity, the fulfillment of human parts in relation to the wholeness of reality. In this aiming, the artist in morality finds satisfaction in steps of progress taken, but also recognizes that it is the nature of human life to keep striving after distant and unattained goals. God is experienced as the lure to go beyond self, to enter larger worlds of thought, feeling, action, and meaning. A morality of wholeness celebrates the possibilities of each part, each person, each situation in relation to the whole of being.

The contexts in which modern man must make his decisions are often far different from those in other periods of history. In the modern period, nature and man have come to a new status. Nature is perceived in new dimensions of vastness, complexity, potentiality. Man has powers once undreamed of. Under these circumstances, man must rethink his images of the appropriate human style of life. In a time when man understood much less about nature, and when he saw himself as being helpless in the presence of many natural and social realities, attitudes of dependence and resignation seemed most appropriate. In this new day man must accept the fact that power has been thrust upon him. His morality must reflect his changed situation. Modern man's crucial moral decisions often have to do with the use of power. Thus, the situation in which we now find ourselves calls for a morality that celebrates life in its potentialities and wholeness, that recognizes the interplay of limitation and possibility, that accepts responsibility in the exercise of power, aware that freedom and discipline are inextricably interwoven. Morality in this sense is a comprehensive concept. It has to do with the values men seek in all human relationships: person to person, in intimate groups, in institutional life, in work and leisure, in community, national, and international relationships. Morality also has to do with the methods men employ in seeking their values and the instrumentalities they employ.

The contemporary situation calls for a future-oriented morality. History is open-ended. Man as a creature of becoming is ever moving toward a future and the future is ever breaking in upon him. A morality which asks man simply to repeat the experiences of men in the past, or blindly to follow injunctions enshrined in ancient authorities of book or institution, is inadequate in a world which is dynamic, relational, and ever-becoming. The continuing responsible search for new and creative styles of human relating, whereby the deeper and finer possibilities of life are released, must be a part of the emerging morality of our time. To see decision-situations in the context of wholeness is to recognize the claim of the future as well as that of the past. It is to celebrate the dignity, wonder, and possibilities of human existence in the context of an unfolding universe.

Taking God into Account in Decision-Making

A nation-wide survey indicated that most Americans affirm belief in God, variously defined. The same study indicated that many persons have difficulty reporting how their belief in God makes a difference to them in dealing with problems, including those of decision-making. It is this gap between intellectual assent and actual behavior which raises in the minds of some observers the question of the meaningfulness of talk about God.

How, then, is the concept of God as the Wholeness-Reality relevant to moral issues and to the processes of decision-making? What does it mean to take God, the Wholeness-Reality, into account in dealing with these issues?

First, to take God into account is to accept the role of decision-maker as a gift entailing stewardship. Man receives life and the possibility of an increasingly human life from God who is source, grace, and goal. To believe in God is to believe in the goodness and purposefulness of creation. It is to affirm the human venture as part of the divine wholeness. It is to accept the privileges and responsibilities of decision-making as a claim of ultimate importance. To see man as bearer of the image of God is to acknowledge man's distinctive role in the divine processes of creation and re-creation through free decision. To take God into account in one's decision-making is to acknowledge the ultimate and cosmic significance of what it is to be a decision-making creature. It is to respond to the vocation of decision-maker with devotion of heart, soul, strength, and mind.

Second, to take God as the Wholeness-Reality into account in decision-making is to recognize a basic structure of integrity in which man is both judged and undergirded. God as the character of reality in its wholeness undergirds the human enterprise with a divine dependability, but also judges man in the inexorable relationship of actions and consequences. God as the reality conjoining the integrity of the individual with the integrity of other individuals with the integrity of the whole provides limits within which man can function creatively, but also frees man for relationships of growing meaning. To take God into account in decision-making is to recognize that man's best judgment and most creative efforts stand under the judgment of a goodness and integrity which never fail. It is to live and work and struggle in the confidence that comes from knowing there are patterns of both growth and decay, health and sickness to which man can relate. Because God is real, the seeds of destruction are in life-styles of irrationalism, hatred, and exploitation; because God is real, the seeds of renewal and hope are in life-styles of inquiry, goodwill, life-affirmation, service, experimentation, and cooperation. To take God into account is to be guided by these considerations in one's decision-making. The awareness of a pervasive integrity introduces a dimension of ultimate importance to the consideration of appropriate goals and values for human life.

Third, to take God into account in decision-making is to reckon with God's work of whole-making in the world. The creative, re-creative, redemptive, whole-making work of God is continuous, ever-moving toward the realization of possibilities in persons, relationships, and situations. To take God into account in decision-making is to seek to bring sensitivity, loving concern, and openness to possibilities for growth in each situation; it is to bear witness to the reality of hope in the specific moment and occasion; it is to keep alive the possibility of reconstruction, rehabilitation, redemption in one's deciding. To take God into account is to affirm one's commitment to the reality which moves toward human completion and fulfillment as one decides for that which encourages fulfillment and wholeness. It is to align oneself in decision-making with the humanizing work of God in the world. It is to declare the glory of God by affirming the ultimate significance of freeing man to be courageously, sensitively, lovingly, usefully human.

The wholeness toward which God keeps moving is not static perfection. It involves creative interchange and intercommunication in the midst of the movement of life. It involves the health which inheres in freedom of interaction among a diversity of parts. It involves the growth which is possible only where there is creative tension. God as the Wholeness-Reality is the basic condition whereby man may move toward the fulfillment of his human destiny in the midst of ambiguities and tensions and complex issues through the exercise of responsible decision.

To take God into account is to take the risks of responsible decision-making in the confidence that by the grace of God a life of moral sensitivity is possible. It is to take these risks in the faith that in the midst of the inevitable mistakes of man there is divine healing and renewal. The God of judgment is also the God of grace.

A Morality Appropriate to the Nature of Man

Human life is fulfilled in the movement toward maturity in humanness. Modern man's need is for a morality which links the perspective of reality in its wholeness, the vision of God at work making for wholeness, and a profound understanding of man as the thinking, feeling, deciding, relating creature whose destiny is fulfilled in being true to his deepest nature. A new day will break in the history of man as he discovers more fully a morality which is grounded in the fundamental realities of God and man. Such a morality is a morality of life celebration.

A morality which is true to the nature of man recognizes that man is a whole creature, with body, mind, spirit amazingly related with each other and with an environing, resonant universe. A truly human morality seeks an appropriate balance in the functioning of the varied dimensions of man's being. Such a morality recognizes that man is both limited and potential. It is concerned with encouraging man to take the next step which can be taken, as he moves toward long-range goals.

At the heart of life is the persistent urge for expression and fulfillment. A truly human ethic reflects that fundamental urge, first, by clarifying appropriate directions for human striving; and second, by clarifying the limitations and disciplines which are inherent in true freedom. Mature morality is positive rather than negative, but it recognizes that the price of excellence is discipline, and maturity in humanness comes by way of disciplined devotion.

Man by nature is a relational creature. The greatest human tragedies occur when things go wrong in man's relationships with self, with fellow human beings, with the eventfulness of the world, with God. The greatest human fulfillments come through creative, redemptive, enriching relationships. A morality which is true to the nature of relational man focuses on what is happening in relationships. Practices and policies and programs are evaluated on a moral basis in terms of their influence on how men relate to themselves, to one another, to their institutions, their families, their communities, their work. In an age of technology, attention to the relational character of man becomes a matter of increasing importance. Enlightened morality resists the pressures upon man to regress into the role of clod or cog, and encourages him to affirm his human role.

Within man are the ambivalent desires for security and adventure. A morality of life-affirmation recognizes both. It seeks the increase of those values through which man comes to feel at home in his universe, but it also keeps alive the vision of the unattained goal, of the good not yet achieved, of the future not yet claimed. Thus, a truly human morality stands in judgment upon an unexamined respectability which stifles creativity. It encourages the will to inquire, to explore, to create, to go beyond where one is, to inhabit an expanding universe of mind and heart and purpose.

Man is a creature endowed with the capacity to choose for integrity. In the exercise of that capacity lies the splendor of the human role, for integrity in self and in relationships is the meaning of wholeness.

To opt for the life of integrity is to affirm that if life is worth living it is worth living well. And if life is to be lived well it must be lived in appreciation of that which gives life depth and qualitative richness, and in pursuit of that which enlarges the world of meaning for increasing numbers of men. The life well lived involves enjoyment in being oneself as the unpurchasable person, in maturity of conscience, in sensitivity to the humanness of others, and in feeling the sheer wonder of existence. It involves the decision to link one's life and influence with significant values and causes, to identify with "those who bear the mark of pain" that one may also identify with those who know the joy of life in its fullness. The life well lived is a life of wakefulness to the present moment and to the new day struggling to be born. It is the life which affirms progression over shrinking back, love over hate, responsible independence over dependence, but which also recognizes that man achieves only in part. It reflects the wisdom that the story of any man's life is measured in the direction of his striving even more than in the sum total of his achievements, in the private victories of the inner life even more than in conspicuous accomplishments, in the capacity to think and imagine and laugh and love and grieve even more than in the capacity to win victories in games in which someone else must lose.

A morality true to the nature of man is celebration in deed and decision-making of the dignity and wonder of the human role. It is witness in concrete deed to the personal decision that life shall be well lived. It is affirmation of the reality of God as creator of that human being who is called to share in the divine work of creation and whole-making.

21.
Challenge to the Churches

IT IS NO SECRET that the organized church has been subjected to increasing criticism in recent years. It is charged with being irrelevant, failing to communicate, being preoccupied with its own internal well-being, failing to bring an authentic witness to its own gospel at crucial points of need within the world. That the church has meant and is meaning a great deal to many persons is obvious. Yet the criticisms persist and the church responds in varied ways, sometimes defensively, sometimes with a call for renewal.

It may be that the current criticism will turn out to be a blessing in disguise. The church is being forced to think in greater depth about its nature and function and to define itself with increasing care. Some of the more vocal critics of the church are not specific about what the church should be doing in order to be relevant. Unfortunately, considerable uncertainty of purpose is manifest within the denominations and local churches themselves. Thus, the churches are now challenged to deal forthrightly with their own "identity crisis" and to declare what distinctive role they propose to enact with excellence.

Some persons think the church is relevant if it simply provides settings for enjoyable social occasions. Others define relevance in terms of meeting psychological needs: for security, reassurance, renewal, recognition, a sense of personal worth. Some take a more sociological approach, holding that the church should function in giving force to social norms, celebrating the values of the group or community. There are many persons who believe the church is enacting its primary role when it is functioning as an agent of social criticism and social change.

Obviously there are many human needs and many values. The question is not simply "Is the church doing something worthwhile?" The question is whether the church has a distinctive role. Is there something the church is called to say or do or be which defines its distinctive function? To put it another way, is there among men the need for a *religious* function, a function involving particular learnings and experiences, knowledges and skills, not being dealt with directly by other agencies in society? If the answer is "yes," the church has its work cut out for it. If the answer is "no," it would be well to acknowledge the implications of this conclusion. In any event, the current discussion of the relevance or irrelevance of the church cannot be significantly productive until the central question of religious function is raised. No one is in a position to pass judgment on the relevance of the church until he is prepared to define and defend some basis on which relevance is to be determined.

The Church in Theological Perspective

In Chapters Three and Four various theories of the nature and function of religion were considered. Attention was called to the historic roles of religion in providing an ultimate "frame of orientation and object of devotion" whereby men find heightened morale and motivation, and in providing symbols through which men affirm and enact shared values, purposes, and commitments in response to the divine. In the idea of God, religion introduces the dimension of ultimacy and calls man to a hope which transcends the frustrations of temporal existence. Religion is that way of life in which man finds his ultimate hope in God.

In Chapters Nine, Ten, and Sixteen consideration was given to the Christian faith and way of life. Christianity shares with other religions in presenting a view of reality expressed in doctrine, myth, sacred story, and drama. It also shares with other religions in providing symbolic rites and acts of devotion in which persons are enabled to affirm and enact the values and commitments called forth by the vision of the divine. Judaism and Christianity affirm the revelation of God as creative power and purposiveness in nature and history. Christianity goes on to affirm God's supreme act of revelation and redemption in Jesus Christ, whereby man is given to know that the God of creative power is also the God of redeeming love. Christianity points to the revealing person and to the witnessing-serving-reconciling community of faith in declaring the good news of the new life God offers man in Christ. The varied doctrines and rites of Christian faith reflect the vision of God which is the distinctive witness of the followers of Jesus Christ.

The question of the church's relevance must ultimately be asked from the theological perspective. The question of the relevance of the *Christian* church is the question of the integrity with which it witnesses to its own vision of God and man. It is the question of the religious relevance of its witness for men who daily cope with the issues of human existence. Obviously the church is irrelevant if man's need for a creative orientation to reality in its wholeness has ceased to exist, or if concern for the vision of God is meaningless. But there is much evidence from history and contemporary experience that this need persists. And the religious function is of crucial importance so long as man asks the ultimate questions pertaining to the meaning of his existence and struggles for a fuller understanding of his destiny in relation to reality in its depths and wholeness. Insofar as the Christian vision does indeed illuminate the human situation with insights and truths of ultimate significance, the Christian church has a clearly defined responsibility. It is called to communicate its vision, to bear witness to it in word and deed and relationship, to interpret its meaning for the problems and possibilities of life. It is called to provide men with those symbols, languages, experiences, and instrumentalities through which faith may be expressed, nurtured, and shared. No other institution assumes this particular responsibility. If there is no vital church, the human race will suffer at the point of its most precious possession—the vision by which it lives. Men require the undergirding, direction, and motivation which religion affords.

Gods there will be, for men must worship. Rites there will be, for man acts out his visions and values in symbolic form. The Judeo-Christian tradition offers distinctive light and wisdom. In varied languages the Judeo-Christian tradition has declared the reality of the God who makes for wholeness and calls man to a new life of wholeness and of hope. The modern world is in need of such a vision and of this call. The church is now challenged to see its role more clearly and to enact it with confidence and excellence. Man is a creature who comes alive through the visions by which he lives. The vision of wholeness and an understanding of its meaning for the contemporary world is sorely needed. The church is called to a new response to its own high calling.

What, then, do we ask of the church in our time? Fundamentally, we ask that it be the church, fulfilling with integrity and excellence those functions which are fundamental to the life of religion and which reflect the wisdom of its particular tradition. More specifically, we say to the church in this time: Give us your vision or revelation, give us a history, and then give us a witness to the vision and to the history in languages which lead us toward humanness and hope in this day.

We Ask of the Church: Its Vision

First, we say to the church: Give us your vision, your revelation of God and man and life. Help us see the dimensions of transcendence and depth and height in the midst of the present moment. Communicate this vision in such a way that it comes, not as a series of intellectual propositions to be accepted, but as light, disclosing the sheer wonder of the universe and human life and all that partakes in being. Give us a vision that will make us ever discontented with a life of triviality, insensitivity, mediocrity. Give us a vision of greatness which calls us out of apathy, which shakes us into the awareness that we have not been born for ease but for a measure of greatness, sharing in the divine work of creation and whole-making in human relations.

We say to the church: Lead us into a worship which is more than a formal exercise remote from life; lead us into a worship which is a celebration of life in its heights and depths, in its joys and sorrows, in its victories and defeats, in its challenge to create a new future; a worship which is life in praise of God.

We say to the church: Be less concerned about theological orthodoxy or with having everyone think alike, and be more concerned with nurturing the sensitive spirit, with helping us see and feel reality in the dimensions of depth and profundity and sanctity; expose us to more persons who communicate a kindling quality and who feel the excitement of being humanly alive.

We are told that the creative power of God is revealed in nature and history and that the redeeming love of God is revealed in Christ. But how often this affirmation comes through like a proposition to be memorized, a statement the church is expected to make! Let it come through as the greatest good news man has ever heard—a vision by which to walk, a light and promise in which to live and die, a summons by which to be stirred. Give us a guiding vision as men seek peace, interdependence, and a community of the truly human.

We Ask of the Church: A History

The whole person requires a tradition or heritage of shared values and purposes. Each of us needs to know who he is in relation to some company of persons with whom he identifies and of whom he seeks to be worthy in the testing times of life. We need a history.

Winston Churchill said that ultimately people are governed by external force or by tradition. To be governed by tradition is not to be oriented toward the past, but it is to receive from the past as one moves into a new future. It is to recognize the interrelatedness of past, present, and future. It is to recognize that man is a part of a web of life. It is to be self-disciplined through devotion to values one has internalized and made his own from his history even as one accepts the responsibility of personal decision in a new situation.

A person may participate in several histories related to family, work, school, community, nation. But more ultimate than these histories is the history of a people who see their lives in relation to God, the God of all families and vocations, communities, nations, and cultures; the God of the present in which the peoples of the earth are struggling to find what it is to be humanly alive; the God of all futures. We say to the church: Reveal to us a history of men who perceive themselves as a people of God, called to his service, judged in his righteousness, renewed in his goodness and summoned to live in the light of his reality. Make clear how this history is still in the making, and how contemporary man can find himself in relation to it.

The Christian says to his church: Provide a more vital ministry of education. It is not enough to provide facts about the Judeo-Christian tradition, although information about events and persons is needed. There is need for an imaginative education which enables persons to enter this history, to appropriate it as their own, to come to a new self-understanding through it. The church is asked to show how Bible, church history, theology, social service, and action in the name of Christ are all witnesses to man's search for a meaningful faith in response to the vision of the God who makes for wholeness. The Christian says to his church: Provide an education which helps us see that our history is open-ended, ever moving into new situations and new days; help us understand how we are called to extend that history, sharing in God's humanizing work; give us this deeper and fuller orientation to life; give us a history through which we may participate more fully in the wholeness of reality.

We Ask of the Church: A Language

Persons grow in humanness in communication, in giving and receiving through varied languages. The life of faith is nurtured in a fellowship of persons in communication pertaining to values and purposes of ultimate concern. Thus, we say to the church: Help us to be more articulate persons in matters of faith; give us languages through which we are enabled to speak of God in human life today.

We are able to talk to each other about likes and dislikes in food, television programs, public figures, and so on. Unfortunately, we are less able to communicate on a thinking, feeling, valuing, aspiring level in matters of enduring importance. We are inwardly impoverished because of this fact.

Historically, religion has offered men varied languages pointing to the dimensions of ultimacy, transcendence, and wholeness: doctrine, the sacred drama of creation and redemption portrayed in art and literature, the gripping metaphor and symbol and parable transmitting the vision and wisdom of the faith. Religion speaks in the language of ritual in which the pivotal experiences of life—birth, growth, marriage, work, play, love, suffering, death, renewal—are recognized, celebrated, and dedicated in the context of faith.

Unfortunately, today these languages often go unlearned and uninterpreted. We sometimes cling to obsolete languages. Persons, even within the church, often become inarticulate in the areas which give life its deepest meaning. Thus, there is need for a religious education which initiates persons into the languages of mature faith. There is need within the churches for humanizing communication, in which persons truly meet as human beings in the sharing of perspectives, concerns, and commitments. Martin Buber once observed that "all real living is meeting." Unfortunately, we have many meetings in which we do not truly meet as human beings.

The contemporary religious situation is complicated by the fact that many of the more familiar religious symbols are associated with situations which no longer exist or which are fast disappearing. Technology and urbanization are changing our ways of thinking and our ways of life. Languages reflecting prescientific or frontier or pastoral or rural settings communicate with fewer and fewer persons. Lacking a theological language with which they can identify, some say that God is dead; others fail to speak of theological matters at all. We ask the church to interpret its symbols, showing their contemporary relevance. We ask the church to be open to new forms of expression. We ask the church to probe present experience in the quest for languages that speak to contemporary man of wholeness and hope and new life in community. We ask the church to be open to the values in a growing body of literature, from many cultures, communicating the universal elements in the heart of man. We ask the church to give us images of maturity and wholeness relevant to all races and nations, to be receptive to the contributions of scholar and saint, artist and scientist, philosopher and man of action.

The communication going on in a church that is living and relevant expresses the church's concern for worship and devotion, for nurture in the life of faith, for pastoral care, for responsible decision-making, and for guidance in the life of wholeness in the world. Thus, we ask the church to give primary attention to these matters, providing knowledge and skills with which persons can speak and act in the light of their vision, their history, and the call of God's future.

It is not enough for the contemporary church to teach general religious and moral principles. Life is lived in the concrete. Thus, we ask the church to provide education in decision-making, helping persons relate the light and wisdom of their faith to the complex personal and social issues in which they are involved. The languages of faith in this day must have communicating value in situations where persons are wrestling with the most difficult problems of life. No other institution in society assumes the explicit responsibility for declaring the reality of God and interpreting the meaning of God's wholeness for the life of men and nations.

Thus we say to the church: In giving us a vision and a history, give us languages whereby the wholeness of the vision may be expressed, nurtured, and mediated. The living church is a communicating church.

We Ask of the Church: A Witness

Above all else, the church in this time is asked to be an authentic witness to the greatness of its vision and the greatness of its hope. In the current confusions of the world there are many witnesses to the irrational, destructive, and immature dimensions of man. The church serves the world exceedingly well when it bears witness to the God who makes for wholeness, and to man as a creature who is born for wholeness. The church serves in bearing witness to the dignity and strengths and possibilities of man.

A part of the church's witness must be in its own internal life. To worship and study and serve and to be in communication pertaining to matters of life's deepest meaning is to bear a mighty witness. To be a remembering, rejoicing, redeeming fellowship, calling all sorts and conditions of men to a new life and hope, is to render a service of inestimable importance. To keep affirming that a life of faith and hope and love is the birthright of every human being is to feed the spirit of man and give direction to the human enterprise. In acknowledging its own shortcomings, and in seeking a continuing reformation and renewal, the church demonstrates its integrity of purpose. In the midst of the criticisms being levelled against it, it is encouraging to see much soul-searching going on within the church. Many churchmen genuinely desire renewal in the church and are prepared to work for it.

However, the most significant changes now to be observed in the church do not have to do with its internal life alone. They have to do with the church's relationship with the secular order. The church which has long declared that *God's supreme language is that of being present with man* is now demonstrating a new determination to implement that teaching in the realities of the world.

The church cannot do everything. Much of the humanitarian work of the world must be done through individuals and various agencies. And yet, it is not enough for the church to speak in words alone. Its most eloquent language is in the caring which seeks out the lost and lone and estranged, in action speaking its word of acceptance and of hope. At the heart of Christian faith is the affirmation of a divine grace which goes forth at personal cost to save and heal and restore and make whole. The church is asked to give witness in deed to this gospel at crucial points within the world, where life is struggling for justice, understanding, integrity, and meaning. In the past the church has demonstrated needs in the area of social service. In due time communities have taken over many of these responsibilities. On a more fundamental level the church is now asked to bear witness to its own gospel, that God calls *all* men to wholeness, and that man himself is often the mediator of God's grace. The ministry of the laity has become the growing edge of the church's life in the secular order. The clergyman has distinctive responsibilities in the gathered church as liturgist, preacher, teacher, administrator, organizer, and pastor. An extremely important function is that of nurturing the priesthood of all believers, sharing in education of laymen for ministry in the world. The laity of the church are called to be the church scattered, the church in the world, bearing witness to the gospel of life in the various structures of society. The whole church is called to be in mission in response to the God who addresses man, not only out of the past and present, but out of a future for which man himself has great responsibility. The witness of its own life and ministry is the church's most eloquent language.

Can modern man speak meaningfully of the reality of God? The answer to this question cannot come in words alone. It must come in the decision for meaning and purposefulness which men bring to their existence. It must come in the trust and devotion men reveal in their daily living. It must come in the celebration of life in its wholeness, which is the worship of God. For many persons the answer will be profoundly influenced by the church's witness to the gospel with which it has been entrusted. It is the enduring function of the church to make God real to man.

REFERENCES AND ACKNOWLEDGMENTS

References and Acknowledgments

The author is grateful for the use of the material quoted or referred to in the text, as listed below.

CHAPTER 1. THE WHOLE PERSON ASKS THE GOD-QUESTION

[1] Margaret Mead, "A New Control of Destiny." *This I Believe*, Edward P. Morgan, ed. (New York, Simon and Schuster, Inc., 1952), p. 116.

[2] Erik H. Erikson, "Eight States of Man." *Childhood and Society* (New York, W. W. Norton and Co., 1950), Chapter 7.

[3] Ernst Bloch, *Das Prinzip der Hoffnung* (Berlin, Suhrkampf Verlag, 1954).

[4] Gordon Allport, *Becoming* (New Haven, Yale University Press, 1955), p. 98.

CHAPTER 2. THE EXPERIMENT OF GETTING ALONG WITHOUT GOD

[1] Corliss Lamont, *The Philosophy of Humanism* (New York, Frederick Ungar Publishing Co., Inc., 1965), p. 14. Used by permission of the author.

[2] Bertrand Russell, "A Free Man's Worship." *Selected Papers of Bertrand Russell*, pp. 14-15, 1927. Used by permission of the publishers, George Allen & Unwin, London.

[3] Among the books appearing in this period were *Humanism States Its Case* (J.A.F.C. Auer), *The Quest of the Ages* (A. E. Haydon), *The Modern Temper* (J. W. Krutch), *A Preface to Morals* (Walter Lippmann), *The Mystery of Religion* (E. D. Martin), *Things and Ideals* and *Natural Laws and Human Hopes* (M. C. Otto), *Humanism* (C. W. Reese), *Religion Coming of Age* (R. W. Sellars).

[4] Max C. Otto, *Things and Ideals* (New York, Holt, Rinehart & Winston, Inc., 1924, 1952), pp. 287-88. Used by permission of the publishers.

[5] R. W. Sellars, "Religious Humanism." *The New Humanist*, May-June, 1933, p. 12. Used by permission of the publisher, Humanist House.

[6] R. W. Sellars, *The Next Step in Religion* (New York, The Macmillan Company, 1918), p. 212.

[7] John Dewey, *A Common Faith* (New Haven, Yale University Press, 1934), p. 27.

[8] *Ibid.*, p. 43.

[9] *Ibid.*, p. 51.

[10] Hazel Barnes, *Humanistic Existentialism* (Lincoln, University of Nebraska Press, 1959), p. 3.

[11] From *The Gospel of Christian Atheism*, by Thomas J. J. Altizer. (The Westminster Press. Copyright © 1963, W. L. Jenkins.) Used by permission.

[12] *Ibid.*, p. 86f.

[13] *Ibid.*, p. 156f.

[14] *Ibid.*, p. 157.

[15] Gabriel Vahanian, *The Death of God* (New York, George Braziller, Inc., 1961), p. 230.

[16] Thomas J. J. Altizer and William Hamilton, *Radical Theology and the Death of God* (Indianapolis, The Bobbs-Merrill Company, Inc., 1966), p. 41.

[17] J. H. Randall, Jr., "The Meaning of Religion for Man." *Preface to Philosophy*, W. P. Tolley, ed. (New York, The Macmillan Company, 1946), pp. 367-368. Used by permission of the publisher.

Chapter 3. Beyond Humanism: Human Hope and the Vision of God

[1] From *Language and Faith; Studies in Sign, Symbol, and Meaning,* by John A. Hutchison (The Westminster Press. Copyright © 1963, W. L. Jenkins), p. 231. Used by permission.

[2] E. A. Burtt, *Man Seeks the Divine* (New York, Harper and Brothers, 1957), p. 33ff.

[3] Gordon Allport, *The Individual and His Religion* (New York, The Macmillan Company, 1950), p. 63. Used by permission of the publisher.

[4] William James, *The Varieties of Religious Experience* (New York, Longmans, Green, and Co., 1916), p. 37.

[5] George Santayana, *The Life of Reason* (New York, Charles Scribner's Sons, 1951), p. 6.

[6] W. H. Bernhardt, A *Functional Philosophy of Religion* (Denver, The Criterion Press, 1958), p. 157. Used by permission of the author.

[7] Isaiah 6:1-8.

[8] Alfred North Whitehead, *Adventures of Ideas* (New York, The Macmillan Company, 1933), p. 41. Used by permission of the publisher.

Chapter 4. The Future of Religion

[1] Some works which may prove helpful in understanding Bonhoeffer are as follows: Dietrich Bonhoeffer, *Prisoner for God: Letters and Papers from Prison* (1953); *The Communion of Saints* (1960); *Act and Being* (1961); *The Cost of Discipleship* (1963); and *Ethics* (1965).

[2] From *Mirror for Man,* by Clyde Kluckhohn (New York, Whittlesey House, 1949), p. 282. Used by permission of McGraw-Hill Book Company.

[3] See the following books by Pierre Teilhard de Chardin: *The Phenomenon of Man* (1959), and *The Divine Milieu* (1960).

[4] Margaret Mead, "A New Control of Destiny." *This I Believe*, Edward P. Morgan, ed. (New York, Simon and Schuster, Inc., 1952), p. 116.

[5] From *Mirror for Man*, by Clyde Kluckhohn (New York, Whittlesey House, 1949), pp. 280, 282, 283. Used by permission of McGraw-Hill Book Company.

[6] Gardner Murphy, *Human Potentialities* (New York, Basic Books, Inc., 1958), pp. 12, 325.

[7] Gardner Murphy, *Personality: A Biosocial Approach to Origins and Structure* (New York, Harper and Brothers, 1947), p. 21.

[8] Julian Huxley, *Religion without Revelation* (New York, Harper and Brothers, 1957), p. 211. Used by permission of Harper & Row, Publishers, Inc.

[9] Alfred North Whitehead, *Science and the Modern World* (New York, The Macmillan Company, 1929), p. 275. Used by permission of the publisher.

Chapter 5. Major Obstacles to Belief in God

[1] C. E. M. Joad, *The Present and Future of Religion* (London, Ernest Benn, Ltd., 1930), p. 108.

[2] *See* Wallace I. Matson, *The Existence of God* (Cornell University Press, 1965); H. J. Paton, *The Modern Predicament* (The Macmillan Company, 1955); R. W. Hepburn, *Christianity and Paradox* (Franklin Watts, 1958).

[3] Alfred North Whitehead, *Religion in the Making* (New York, The Macmillan Company, 1926), p. 77.

[4] Harold K. Schilling, *Science and Religion* (New York, Charles Scribner's Sons, 1962), p. 22f.

Chapter 6. Reformulating the God-Question

[1] Dietrich Bonhoeffer, *The Cost of Discipleship* (New York, The Macmillan Company, 1949), p. 15.

Chapter 7. An Appropriate Agnosticism

[1] Karl Barth, *The Word of God and the Word of Man,* Douglas Horton, trans. (London, The Pilgrim Press, 1928), p. 186.

[2] Carl Michalson, "The Real Presence of the Hidden God." *Faith and Ethics,* Paul Ramsey, ed. (New York, Harper and Brothers, 1957), p. 245.

[3] A perceptive study of certain aspects of the doctrines of the hiddenness and openness of God by Robert C. Coburn, "The Hiddenness of God and Some Barmecidal God Surrogates," appeared in *The Journal of Religion,* October 27-November 10, 1960 (Vol. LVII, pp. 22-23).

[4] Harlow Shapley, *Of Stars and Men,* p. 149. Reprinted by permission of the Beacon Press, copyright © 1958 by Harlow Shapley.

[5] Gordon Allport, *The Individual and His Religion* (New York, The Macmillan Company, copyright 1950), p. 138. Used by permission of the publisher.

Chapter 8. The Strange and Varied Languages of Faith

[1] Paul Van Buren, *The Secular Meaning of the Gospel* (New York, The Macmillan Company, 1963), p. xiv.

[2] *Ibid.,* p. 79.

[3] Paul Tillich, "Introduction." *The Grandeur and Misery of Man,* by David E. Roberts (New York, Oxford University Press, 1955), p. vi.

[4] Samuel H. Miller, *The Dilemma of Modern Belief* (New York, Harper & Row, Publishers, Inc., 1963), pp. 7-8. Used by permission of the publishers.

Chapter 9. The Christian Vision of God

[1] George Santayana, *The Life of Reason* (New York, Charles Scribner's Sons, 1951), p. 5. Used by permission of the publishers.

Chapter 10. Christian Imagery: Resource and Stumbling Block

[1] Frederick Ferré, *Language, Logic and God* (New York, Harper and Brothers, 1961), p. 164. Used by permission of Harper & Row, Publishers, Inc.

[2] Alfred North Whitehead, *Adventures of Ideas* (New York, The Macmillan Company, 1933), pp. 213, 214. Used by permission of the publisher.

[3] Amos Wilder, *Otherworldliness and the New Testament* (New York, Harper and Brothers, 1954), pp. 22-23. Used by permission of Harper & Row, Publishers, Inc.

Chapter 11. Can New Ground Be Broken in Theology?

[1] Alfred North Whitehead, *Science and the Modern World* (New York, The Macmillan Company, 1929), p. 270. Used by permission of the publisher.

[2] C. A. Coulson, "Protestant Thought and Natural Science—A Review Article," *The Drew Gateway*, Winter, 1961, p. iii. Used by permission of the publisher.

[3] For an elaboration of this thesis see the author's article, "Science and Religion: Has the Conflict Been Resolved?" in *Religion in Life*, Winter, 1962-63.

[4] Harlow Shapley, *Of Stars and Men* (Boston, Beacon Press, Inc.). Reprinted by permission of the Beacon Press, copyright © 1958 by Harlow Shapley.

[5] Harvey Cox, *The Secular City* (New York, The Macmillan Company, 1965), p. 2.

[6] J. A. T. Robinson, *Christian Morals Today* (Philadelphia, Westminster Press, 1964), p. 20.

Chapter 12. Affirming the Reality of God: Four Contemporary Approaches

[1] Nels F. S. Ferré, *Searchlights on Contemporary Theology* (New York, Harper and Brothers, 1961), p. 84. Used by permission of Harper & Row, Publishers, Inc.

[2] Nels F. S. Ferré, *The Christian Understanding of God* (New York, Harper and Brothers, 1951), pp. 15-16. Used by permission of Harper & Row, Publishers, Inc.

[3] *Ibid.*, p. 35.

[4] Nels F. S. Ferré, *Searchlights on Contemporary Theology* (New York, Harper and Brothers, 1961), p. 84. Used by permission of Harper & Row, Publishers, Inc.

[5] Nels F. S. Ferré, *The Christian Understanding of God* (New York, Harper and Brothers, 1951), p. 105. Used by permission of Harper & Row, Publishers, Inc.

[6] Nels F. S. Ferré, *Searchlights on Contemporary Theology* (New York, Harper and Brothers, 1961), pp. 81, 133. Used by permission of Harper & Row, Publishers, Inc.

[7] Nels F. S. Ferré, "Does Man Really Want Peace?" *Saturday Review*, July 1, 1967, pp. 11-12.

[8] Nels F. S. Ferré, *The Christian Understanding of God* (New York, Harper and Brothers, 1951), p. 222. Used by permission of Harper & Row, Publishers, Inc.

[9] Paul Tillich, *Systematic Theology I* (Chicago, The University of Chicago Press, 1951), pp. 205, 235, 237, 238, 239. Used by permission of the publisher.

[10] *Ibid.*, p. 49.

[11] Paul Tillich, *Systematic Theology II* (Chicago, The University of Chicago Press, 1957), p. 115. Used by permission of the publisher.

[12] John Macquarrie, *Principles of Christian Theology* (New York, Charles Scribner's Sons, 1966), p. 98.

[13] *Ibid.*, p. 103.

[14] *Ibid.*, p. 110.

[15] Rudolph Bultmann, "Bultmann Replies to His Critics." *Kerygma and Myth*, Hans Bartsch, ed. (London, S. P. C. K.), pp. 197, 198. Used by permission of the publisher.

[16] Rudolph Bultmann, "The Idea of God and Modern Man." *Translating Theology into the Modern Age*, Robert W. Funk, ed. (New York, Harper & Row, Publishers, Inc., 1965), p. 94. Used by permission of the publishers.

[17] H. N. Wieman, *Man's Ultimate Commitment* (Carbondale, Ill., Southern Illinois University Press, 1958), p. 11.

[18] *Ibid.*, p. 12.

[19] H. N. Wieman, *The Source of Human Good* (Chicago, The University of Chicago Press), pp. 38-39. Copyright 1946 by H. N. Wieman. Used by permission of the author.

[20] Schubert M. Ogden, *The Reality of God* (New York, Harper & Row, Publishers, Inc., 1966), p. 37.

CHAPTER 13. TOWARD A THEOLOGY OF HOPING

[1] An insightful analysis of hope is found in William F. Lynch's *Images of Hope* (Helicon Press, 1965). A number of suggestions have been drawn from this volume.

[2] James Jeans, *Physics and Philosophy* (New York, The Macmillan Company, 1943), p. 216. Used by permission of the publisher.

CHAPTER 14. GOD AND THE WHOLENESS OF REALITY

[1] Jan Smuts, *Holism and Evolution* (New York, The Macmillan Company, 1926), pp. 86, 87. Used by permission of the publisher.

[2] Harry Overstreet, *The Enduring Quest* (New York, W. W. Norton & Company, Inc., 1931), p. 264.

CHAPTER 15. GOD AS GROUND, GRACE, AND GOAL

[1] Dietrich Bonhoeffer, *Creation and Fall* (London, SCM Press, Ltd., 1959), p. 10. Published in the United States in one volume with *Temptation* by The Macmillan Company.

[2] Ian G. Barbour, *Issues in Science and Religion* (Englewood Cliffs, N. J., Prentice-Hall, Inc., © 1966), p. 458. Used by permission of the publisher.

[3] Philip H. Phenix, *Education and the Worship of God* (Philadelphia, Westminster Press, 1966), pp. 28-29.

Chapter 16. God and the Christian Experience of Hope

[1] Daniel Day Williams, *God's Grace and Man's Hope* (New York, Harper and Brothers, 1949), p. 50. Used by permission of Harper & Row, Publishers, Inc.

Chapter 18. Celebrating Human Dignity in the Midst of Adversity

[1] Quoted in J. S. Bixler, *Education for Adversity* (Cambridge, Mass., Harvard University Press, 1952), p. 27.

[2] Viktor Frankl, *Man's Search for Meaning*, p. 77. Copyright © 1959, 1962 by Viktor Frankl. Reprinted by permission of the Beacon Press.

Chapter 19. The Celebration of Life in Devotion and Prayer

[1] Rufus Jones, *The Flowering of Mysticism; The Friends of God in the Fourteenth Century* (New York, The Macmillan Company, 1931), p. 251.

[2] James Bissett Pratt, *The Religious Consciousness* (New York, The Macmillan Company, 1924), pp. 474-475. Used by permission of the publisher.

[3] William Ernest Hocking, *The Meaning of God in Human Experience* (New Haven, Yale University Press, 1916), p. 427. Used by permission of the publisher.

INDEX

Index

D.

E.

F.

G.

PRINTED IN U.S.A.